RAILWAY RAMBLES

London and the South-East

Clive Higgs

Published by Sigma Leisure – an imprint of
Sigma Press, 1 South Oak Lane, Wilmslow, Cheshire SK9 6AR, England.

British Library Cataloguing in Publication Data
A CIP record for this book is available from the British Library.

ISBN: 1-85058-452-4

Typesetting and Design by: Sigma Press, Wilmslow, Cheshire.

Photographs: the author

Cover photograph: John Byrne of Bromley, Kent

Maps: Jeremy Semmens

Printed by: J.W. Arrowsmith Ltd, Bristol

Disclaimer: the information in this book is given in good faith and is believed to be correct at the time of publication. No responsibility is accepted by either the author or publisher for errors or omissions, or for any loss or injury howsoever caused. Only you can judge your own fitness, competence and experience.

Preface

The pastime of country walking or 'rambling' first became popular in the 1920s when it was popularly known as hiking. This volume, I hope will be of interest to those who have already participated in rambling, and to those who have not. I also hope that the book will appeal to visitors from overseas who most probably in their own countries do not have the facilities of going from A to B without traversing hard roads. One of the unique features of the British Isles is the vast network of public footpaths (rights of way) which enable the traveller to peregrinate from village to village without being disturbed by the sound or smell of passing motor traffic.

A particular feature of this book is that, in the main, the routes are not circular. Many of the books now available giving particulars of country walks assume that the participants will arrive by motor car, in which case the route has to be from the car park and back to the same car park. A circular route of this nature has a disadvantage in that it often means traversing the very same places again on the return journey. By travelling to the beginning of the walk and subsequently returning by rail, it enables the routes to be on a "station to station" basis and if the reader may care to participate in a glass or two of ale on the route, he or she may have no fears about the consequences of driving home.

To the South-East area around London, there is a great variety of scenery, including open downland, heathland, moorland agricultural country, areas which are largely flat and areas which attain heights of almost 1,000 feet.

By following the text for each particular walk, the routes should be largely self-explanatory, and one does not have to be an athlete to participate. The distances covered in each particular walk are between 5½ miles and 8½ miles, and should be within the range of the quite young and the "not so very old". Along most of the routes are places of refreshment where pleasant halts can be made, and there are of course abundant facilities for picnics.

Good walking shoes should be worn at all times and one must bear in mind the fact that the British countryside is apt to be a trifle damp. Even after several weeks of dry weather, one finds that ground can be quite marshy at isolated places.

The routes follow recognised rights of way, and under the new Acts recently passed, it is now mandatory for the land owner to keep these rights of way unimpeded. For example, if a right of way crosses the middle of a cornfield, the farmer now has the obligation to keep the path free of crops, thus avoiding the necessity of having to circum-navigate fields of growing crops as was the case before this new legislation took effect.

In every instance, the starting points and finishing points are at railway stations which have a train service on all seven days of the week*. Do, however, bear in mind that British Rail sometimes under-take essential engineering work at weekends, thus making it desir-able to enquire in advance, or be prepared to face substitute bus services which will lengthen the duration of the journey.

Walking in the countryside is enjoyable all the year round. Many readers will no doubt show a preference for Spring or Summer, but the fields and woods have a charm of their own on a gusty winter's day and even in the shortest days of December, when the distance of each route can be comfortably covered in hours of daylight. Remem-ber too that when the frost lies hard and white on the ground and hedges, Southern England becomes a "winter wonderland" more than worth a visit.

Clive Higgs

As this book goes to press, Great Eastern Railways have announced the complete withdrawal of Sunday services to Chappel and Wakes Colne, so Route 12 should not be undertaken on Sundays or Bank Holidays.

Notes for Walkers

Rights of Way

To the best of the author's knowledge and belief, all the routes follow recognised rights of way as defined in The Ordnance Survey's "Landranger" maps. It may well help if the rambler is in possession at the ·appropriate sheet, as once the art of map-reading is mastered, the possession of such a map can well enhance the pleasure of the outing.

A fact that has to be faced is that rights of way tend to be diverted (sometimes illegally) and others through sheer lack of use become indistinct and difficult to follow. If a reader should accidentally stray from the route and be confronted by the landowner or his representative, courtesy should always prevail typically by a response such as "I am sorry . . . I seem to have strayed from the public footpath . . . can you tell me which way I should have gone?". Remember too that our heritage of public footpaths are public ways but in general go over private property. Due respect should be the order of the day.

A common complaint is caused by the sowing of crops without leaving a "gap" for the footpath. You may well find that it is easier in these circumstances to follow the perimeter of the field, rather than battling through four-feet high corn or, worse still, getting entangled in oil-seed rape! Should you find a path genuinely obstructed, you are legally entitled to "trespass" on private land around the offending portion. In the event of any blatant hindrance such as a barbed-wire fence, it is suggested that you report the facts to the Open Spaces Society of 25a Bell Street, Henley-on-Thames, Oxon, RG9 2BA. This body zealously and non-politically acts as guardian of paths and commons, and a modest annual subscription includes the cost of interesting magazines, etc. Alternatively you could write to The

Ramblers Association of 1/5 Wandsworth Road, London, SW8 2XX who have similar interests.

The Country Code

1. Avoid damage to fences, gates and walls. These are there for a purpose and to repair damage is often expensive.

2. Always close fences and gates to prevent livestock escaping.

3. Keep to footpaths and other rights of way and avoid causing damage to crops.

4. Respect other people's property. Farm machinery is often left unattended, close to where it will be needed, and should therefore, be left untouched.

5. Keep dogs under control and if necessary keep them on a lead. If you cannot control your pet you should not take it out into the countryside. This applies not only where farm livestock is concerned but to many other areas. Rampaging dogs pose a serious threat to deer, especially when they have young, and desertion and even premature abortion sometimes result. Other wild mammals are disturbed as well as ground-nesting and ground-feeding birds.

6. Do not leave litter and especially do not discard lighted cigarettes, matches or anything else that could cause a fire.

7. Drive slowly and safely in the country. Always assume that there might be a herd of cows or a stationary tractor round the next bend.

8. When walking on country roads always remember to keep to the right, in single file.

Contents

Locations of the Walks

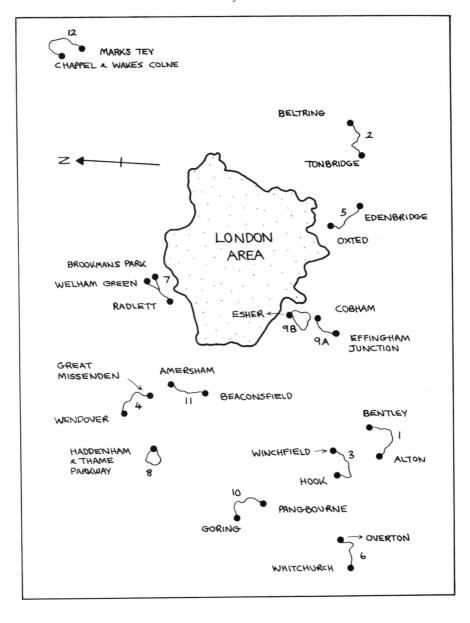

Route 1: The Hangers of Hampshire

Distance: 6½miles

Map: OS Landranger 186

Start: Bentley Station (South Western Trains)

Finish: Alton Station (South Western Trains)

Train service (from Waterloo): hourly

Journey times (minimum): to Bentley (42 miles), 60 minutes; from Alton (46½ miles), 67 minutes

Ticket: Day Return to Alton (available for leaving the train at Bentley on the outward journey)

Introduction

If you consult a dictionary you will find the word "hanger", to have various definitions including "a steeply wooded hillside". In practise this usage of the word appears to be more or less confined to the northern side of the county of Hampshire and indeed one of the recently-introduced long distance footpaths has been entitled "The Hangers Way", a portion of which will be encountered on this particular route.

The town of Alton was once a great centre of the brewing industry and the terrain around used to contain vast areas of hop vines, of which only a few remain. What are still to be seen are the Malt Houses, some adjoining farm houses and some more isolated, and indeed on approaching the village of East Worldham, a substantial building of this nature is seen, now converted to private dwellings as in the case of many of the Oast Houses in Kent, (see Route 2).

The journey starting point at Bentley Station is a matter of a few hundred yards from the River Wey which rises in the Hampshire Hills near Alton and ends at its confluence with the Thames at

Weybridge. The walk encounters gently rising country to the south of the Wey Valley eventually descending back to the "infant" Wey which is crossed by a footbridge shortly before arriving at Alton. Only three villages are encountered on the walk, the first being Binsted set above the valley and containing a fine church. Further signs of habitation are not encountered until the sleepy outpost of Wyck is reached – it is curious that such a remote settlement should exist within 40 miles of Central London.

The third and last of the villages traversed is East Worldham which, unlike its neighbour West Worldham a mile away, at least contains a not unsubstantial inn, and something of an infrequent omnibus service linking the towns of Alton and Petersfield.

The total distance of the walk is about $6\frac{1}{2}$ miles with nothing daunting in the way of hill climbs. At the beginning at Bentley Station there are no facilities for refreshments as the village lies some three-quarters of a mile to the north. Reference is given in the text to the two inns that provide sustenance, i.e. at Binsted (about $2\frac{3}{4}$ miles from the start) and East Worldham ($2\frac{1}{4}$ miles from the finish). At the conclusion of the walk, the town of Alton abounds in pubs and eating houses (the town centre and High Street are a matter of a few hundred yards beyond the Railway station). On the Station itself there are buffets open to all travellers but used mainly by those who congregate here to savour the enjoyment of a ride by steam train, for it is here that the privately-run Mid-Hants railway (commonly known as the "Watercress Line") begins its shuttle over the Hampshire Hills to Alresford and back – a worthwhile and nostalgic journey for which reasonably priced tickets can be purchased from the British Rail booking office at Alton Station.

The train journey from Waterloo takes 60 – 100 minutes according to the time and day of the week. Day return tickets to Alton are of course available to those departing one station short at Bentley and are the most economical purchase.

The Journey

The journey starts at Waterloo Station, and after a few minutes one passes through Clapham Junction dubbed as the "busiest station in the World". Shortly after this comes "sporting" Wimbledon famous not only for its tennis championships but also being the home of the Greyhound Derby, and of a nowadays not unsubstantial football team. The way leads through the residential suburbs of Raynes Park and New Malden, and to the north are the hills of Coombe Woods and Richmond Park. Thence on to Surbiton, one of the "Queens of the suburbs". The peculiar thing about Surbiton is that before the railway came it did not exist. The people of Kingston-upon-Thames a mile or so to the north would have nothing to do with the railway, so therefore it was built through what is now known as Surbiton across open country, and the town of Surbiton grew around the railway!

Vintage London & South Western Railway signal box beautifully preserved at Ash Vale Junction

Beyond, the back gardens became longer, and patches of greenery more frequent. The next station is Esher, set amongst attractive commons, and upon leaving the station on the left-hand side will be seen the famous Sandown Park race course which has high class meetings at regular intervals all the year round. Then come Walton-on-Thames, and Weybridge, Thameside localities, which perhaps have mainly lost their original village character being dormitory suburbs of those who have found prosperity in the City of London. A quarter of a mile past Weybridge, the line crosses the River Wey and a glimpse may be seen on the left of some peculiar concrete banking amongst the trees. This is all that is left of the famous Brooklands motor racing track which in the thirties was the mecca of all those who liked the noises and smells of the internal combustion engine. Passing through Byfleet the country becomes more wooded and one soon arrives at Woking, which is the central town of an administrative district known as Surrey Heath. The town now known as Woking also had a history which is based upon the coming of the railway, the actual village of Woking being about two miles to the south. When the railway came, a new township emerged around the station, and until comparatively recent times, the town which now know as Woking was called Woking Station, as opposed to the village of Woking. This apparent discrepancy was remedied some seventy years ago by calling the new town Woking, and the original village Old Woking.

Evidence of the "Surrey Heath" are soon found upon both sides of the line and the next station is Brookwood. This locality also has sporting connections, as a couple of miles away is Bisley, the mecca of rifle enthusiasts, and the venue of their annual championships. On the left approaching Brookwood Station in a large cemetery. Until pre-war days it was possible to hire a carriage for the coffin and other carriages for the mourners from London (Necropolis) Station which was adjacent to Waterloo, and have a private train to the cemetery. At Pirbright junction one leaves the main line to the south-west and continues across the wild heather and pinewood of Pirbright Common and a short tunnel leads under a sandy range of hills known as the Chobham Ridges. Much of the ground on the left-hand side here is inaccessible, having been taken over by the Ministry of Defence for activities associated with the military. Passing Ash Vale a glimpse will be seen of the renovated Basingstoke Canal, after which the somewhat featureless country of the vale of Blackwater is traversed, and so into Aldershot, with its military associations. The town is now part of a conurbation with the neighbouring localities of Farnborough, and Farnham. On through Farnham, where after a brief incursion into Hampshire, one is back in Surrey and thence back into Hampshire again, with the woodlands of Alice Holt Forest on the left, and into Bentley, where the day's walk starts.

The Walk

Leaving the "down" platform at the rear end of Bentley Station pass through a swing gate and follow a clear path which leads along the right-hand side of a meadow with woods on the right. Continue across a stile and a fence and straight ahead across a further meadow, through a swing gate into a small road. Cross this road to a stile opposite and go forward to a point at the corner of some wooded ground on the right.

Late autumn on a remote Hampshire trackway

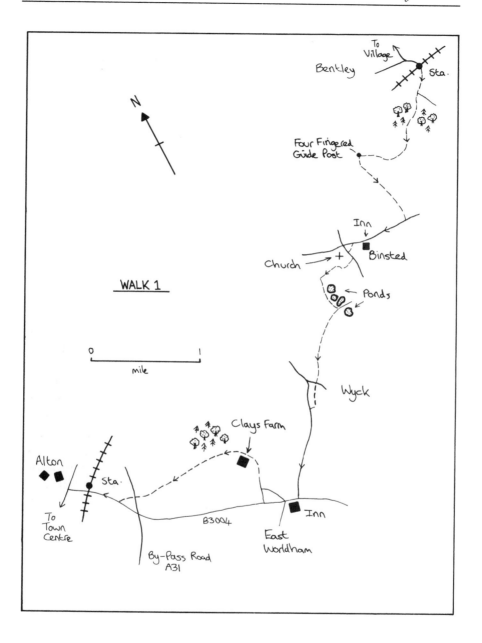

Then, go ahead for about twenty yards and turn right with further woods on the left. After only a few yards, turn left to a path leading into the woods.

The path rises slightly uphill, bearing slightly left and then slightly right through a small clearing, and then uphill via a green track which after a little while has ferns and woods on the right, and coniferous trees on the left. Cross a stile and keep ahead with the woods now on the right ignoring a stile which leads to a path in the woods. Then cross a further stile, keeping to a clear path which runs along the right-hand side of a field, (the woods on the right are on a steep bank and constitute a typical example of a "hanger"). At the end of this field cross a fence (the fence has a stile in it), and over another stile and straight ahead on a clear path which leads over an open field with views of the Wey Valley. As you cross over this large field you will see a four-fingered guide post ahead.

At this guide post, turn left along a clear path which leads across the same field as you were in and runs downhill towards some wooded ground. At the foot of this hill cross a small stream by a wooden footbridge and continue along a clear path. After about only thirty yards, turn left at a footpath sign and enter the woods. This clear path soon crosses a further small stream by a plank bridge and then slightly uphill through the woods (you may have to duck under or climb over a number of tree trunks, because this wood, like many others in the south-east has suffered some damage during the storms of recent years). The path emerges from the wood and continues rising gently uphill at the right-hand side of a field and eventually ignoring the paths and tracks to the right and the left, leads out into a minor road. At this minor road, turn right and after a short half mile you will be in the village of Binsted. On entering the village, The Cedars public house serves amongst other things real ale and good food.

Shortly after passing the public house, turn left at a footpath sign and continue ahead along a clear enclosed path which leads out to another road with the church opposite. Go into the churchyard, continue to its far right-hand corner and then through a gap in a hedge to a path which runs slightly downhill with a hedge on the right.

Where the hedge bears right, turn right onto a farm track and after about twenty yards turn left again continuing downhill on the path which crosses this field. At the end of this field, on approaching a belt of trees turn right for just a few paces and then turn left where the path steeply descends through a belt of trees – a "mini hanger" (take care, the descent is steep and can be overgrown) then over a plank bridge with a three-fingered post ahead. At this point turn left where the path is in the form of a rough track. Continue on this track keeping to the valley floor with a number of artificial ponds on the left. After passing the third pond (with a fourth pond ahead), enter an old sunken lane where you turn right. After a good three-quarters of a mile, you will emerge amongst the scattered dwellings of the village of Wyck. This is a lonely hamlet, with neither church, school, shop nor public house, On reaching a tarmac road, go straight ahead with a large farm building (Wyck Farm House) on your left. After about one hundred yards, turn right and cross a field with a plantation of new trees on the immediate left, through a hollow and straight on with a brick wall on the left, through a swing gate into a drive. Here turn right and emerge through a lodge gate, where you turn left into a minor road. Follow this road onwards for a good mile until reaching the village of East Worldham, where you turn right into the main road. The Three Horseshoes public house ahead serves meals, snacks, and real Hampshire ale.

Opposite the public house is Shelleys Lane. Proceed along this lane and after a short half mile bear right at a junction of lanes and continue forward to a farm (Clays Farm) and after passing the farm buildings on the left, continue ahead on a track which after a brief dip runs ahead to some woods. Here bear left with the woods on the right. At a point some fifty yards ahead the track veers off to the right following the edge of the woods. Here take a signposted path which goes slightly to the left and so across a large field (in the centre of this field is a somewhat lonely guide post which should ensure that you should continue in the right direction). The path which is part of the Hangers Way continues across this large field to a point just to the left of its far right corner. Continue into the next field with a hedge (and another hanger) on the left and the uplands of Neatham Down on the right.

At the far left-hand corner of this field go through a short stretch of undergrowth to the next field where you turn right keeping a straight course across the field under the electricity pylon lines, and so through another stile into the (dual carriageway) Alton by-pass.

WITH GREAT CARE cross the road to the continuation of the path down a bank and across a brick bridge (over the infant River Wey) and via an enclosed path which bears slightly left and comes out into a main road where you turn right and onwards for a short half a mile to Alton Station.

Route 2: The Hop Vines of Kent

Distance: 7 miles

Map: OS Landranger 188

Start: Tonbridge Station (South Eastern)

Finish: Beltring Station (South Eastern)

Outward Train service: from Charing Cross, three per hour Monday to Saturday and two per hour on Sundays

Return Train service: from Beltring, hourly

Journey times (minimum): to Tonbridge 29½ miles, 41 minutes; from Beltring 26½ miles, 58 minutes

Ticket: Day Return to Beltring (available for leaving train at Tonbridge on outward journey)

Introduction

The central part of the County of Kent, i.e. the band of country that runs from east to west between the North and South Downs is broadly described as the Weald. It is in the main a sparsely populated area although some of the villages, particularly those near railway stations have a fair proportion of modern commuter dwellings.

This particular route is in the basin of the River Medway to the east of the large market town of Tonbridge which is the starting point. The growing of hops is still a prominent feature of the agricultural scene in this and some other parts of the county. Evident even now are the Oast Houses which adjoin the farm houses, where the hops are dried in the kilns before being purchased by the brewers. Earlier in the century the hop picking season was a great event in these parts, and train after train used to arrive at country stations with hordes of London families from the poorer parts of the Metropolis to partake in the gathering of the harvest.

The River Medway itself (aptly named as it is virtually the "middle way" through the County) divides what we know as East Kent and West Kent. There is a peculiar legend that inhabitants of the western bank of the river are "Men of Kent" and those of the opposite side "Kentish Men", hence the name of the country inn which the walk passes by shortly before crossing a river at Little Mill. I have earlier referred to the area as being the Medway "basin" – I have particularly used this designation as opposed to the word valley. Hence the walk does not encounter any formidable hill climbs, just a gentle undulation at a point early in the walk where the bank of the river is forsaken in favour of quiet paths which lead to the peaceful village of Golden Green. The total distance covered is in the region of 7 miles. At the very beginning there are abundant facilities for refreshment in the town of Tonbridge, followed on the route by pleasant country inns at Golden Green and Little Mill, the latter being the aforementioned "Man of Kent".

The River Medway and castle at Tonbridge

Thereafter and almost at the end of the journey one encounters the enormous Whitbread Hop Farm with its bars, buffets and restaurant (a place well worth a visit). The final point for sustenance is an inn at the corner of the lane leading to Beltring Station, the station itself being just a "halt" in rural surroundings. Day return tickets to Beltring are of course available for leaving the train at Tonbridge Station on the outward journey. On returning from Beltring you will normally have to change at the next stop (Paddock Wood) for a semi-fast connection back to London.

The Journey

On leaving Charing Cross Station, one is immediately on Hungerford Bridge which spans the River Thames. This is one of the bridges that carry only rail traffic although a lineside footway is available for pedestrians. To the right are views of Westminster with Big Ben, The Abbey and The Houses of Parliament and to the left the skyline of the City itself with St Paul's Cathedral itself prominent in the middle foreground.

Beyond the bridge is the "South Bank" with the Festival Hall on the left and The Victory Arch (the grand main entrance to Waterloo Station) on the right. Waterloo East is the first station to be passed, something of a poor relation to Waterloo itself. An elevated section of the line leads to London Bridge passing the site of the old Hop Exchange where hops from the Kentish countryside used to be auctioned to bidders representing the many brewers that had their establishments in the Central London area.

After London Bridge follows a rather dreary and featureless 3 miles through the flat ground of Southwark and Bermondsey. Before London expanded this was a marshy plain through which the Rivers Neckinger and Effra meandered their way to the Thames. These small streams are now veritably "lost" having been relegated to the status of underground pipes. At New Cross a small ridge forming part of the South London Heights is traversed by a cutting and a short tunnel and at St John's one enters more conventional suburban land. It is at Grove Park that the scenery becomes slightly greener and after passing through a tunnel one encounters the leafy outer suburbs of Elmstead Woods and Chislehurst, the latter being somewhat famous for its caves which were a sheltering place for thousands of South Londoners during the Blitz of 1940/41.

Petts Wood and Orpington follow and then the long climb into the North Downs of Kent begins in earnest, with the rural stations of Chelsfield and Knockholt set in chalky surroundings. The line then burrows deep into the hills and soon enters the 1¼ mile long Polhill Tunnel which marks the beginning of a descent to the valley of the River Darent. The escarpment at Polhill itself seen on the right shortly after emerging from the tunnel became somewhat devastated in the great storm of October 1987 when thousands of acres of woodland were laid waste.

The River Darent itself is crossed soon after passing through Dunton Green Station. It is just a small brook here and the adjacent village is aptly named Riverhead. A further climb into hills now ensues and after passing through Sevenoaks Station one soon disappears into the darkness of Weald Tunnel – over 2 miles long and the longest in South East England. The ridge of hills under which one is passing is the Greensand Hills, a sandy strip of quite high ground between the chalk of the North Downs and the clay of the Weald and the Medway Basin.

The descent continues through the wayside station of Hildenborough and rural (typically "Wealden") scenery abounds for the odd 3 miles to the crossing of the River Medway on the outskirts of Tonbridge Town.

The Walk

Leaving Tonbridge Station at the main entrance, turn left and first right at a roundabout into Vale Road. Continue along this road ignoring turnings to the right and left for a good three-quarters of a mile. This part of the walk leads through a light industrial estate, and just after passing the fire station on the right, and immediately beyond a bridge over the river, turn right at a public footpath sign. This path follows the left-hand bank of the river Medway, eventually (after a good mile) passing under an iron bridge which leads to a sand-pit. Shortly after passing a lock in the river, the path emerges into a small wooded area. Emerging from this and bearing to the left with the line

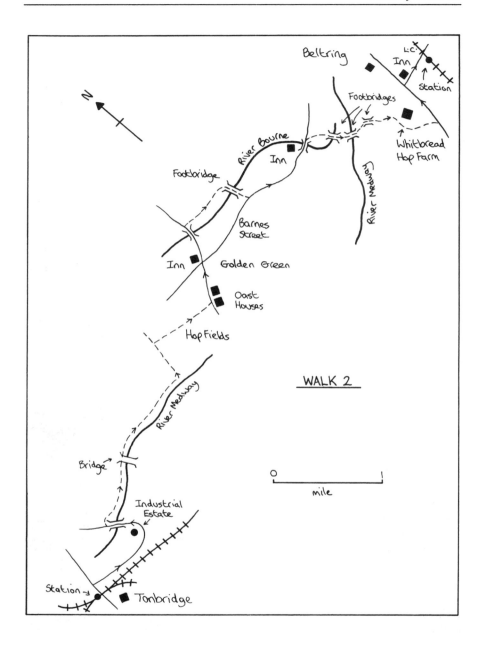

of the river, some 150 yards after leaving the wood turn left along a clear path which runs straight ahead through a gap in the hedge, and onwards over a concrete bridge crossing a water course. The path now becomes a clear track. Where the track bends left near a yellow waymark, continue straight ahead rising very slightly. Reaching a hedge do not go straight ahead but turn sharp right along a path which follows the left-hand side of this field that you have just crossed.

Shortly the hedge bends to the left but at this point keep straight ahead towards the field containing hop poles. Cross over a stile and a small footbridge forward through this hop vine. Ignore a crossing track and continue ahead with a hedge on the right and a continuation of the hop vine on the left. On joining a minor road turn left and continue for a good half mile (with pleasant views of oast houses on the left and right) to a triangular road junction at the village of Golden Green.

At this village, on the left is the friendly "local" – The Bell public house – with a selection of good beers imported from Berkshire and a wide variety of food.

The Bell Inn at Golden Green

After passing or visiting The Bell Inn, turn left along Victoria Road signposted to Hadlow. In a couple of hundred yards or so at the bottom of a slight dip, and after crossing in quick succession two "arms" of the River Bourne, turn right along a path which follows closely the left-hand bank of this tributary of The Medway. A half mile ahead turn right across a footbridge with waymarks with the insignia "WW". This is part of the long distance path, The Wealden Way. Cross a field with a hedge ahead then left at the hedge, following the hedge around to join a secondary road at a locality known as Barnes Street.

Turn left here and continue for the short half mile to the village of Little Mill. Here is another public house, The Man of Kent which serves real Kentish Ales, plus meals and snacks. Immediately after passing or calling at the "Man of Kent", cross a bridge over a small river, and then turn right on a public footpath which runs with the river on the right. Ignore a footbridge on the right, and, after a few yards beyond this footbridge at a junction of paths, fork right with the river continuing on your immediate right. The path joins a track emerging from the left-hand side, where proceed straight ahead through an iron gate, and onwards to a substantial footbridge over the River Medway.

After crossing the footbridge, turn left at a post which is currently waymarked, and with the river on your left to a footbridge and stiles which cross a backwater of the river. At this point continue forward for about 50 yards until a junction of paths is reached, and then turn right, away from the river, with some wooded ground on your left. This path continues straight on and at the end of the field bear slightly to the right with a hedge on the left, and after about 30 yards follow a left-hand path which crosses a plank bridge over a small stream, and over another plank bridge into a large field which is in the grounds of the Whitbread Hop Farm.

Continue straight ahead across this field to a drive with a hop vine on the right-hand side. Keep right, ignoring the car park gate to the left. At the oast houses ahead, turn right, and then left through another car park past a restaurant, and into a junction of main roads at a roundabout. Turn left at the main road (signposted to East

Peckham) and after about a quarter of a mile to another public house, where you turn down a minor road to the right (signposted to the station), and so to Beltring Station for the return journey home.

Route 3: The Basingstoke Canal

Distance: 7¾ miles

Map: OS Landranger 186

Start: Winchfield Station (South Western Trains)

Finish: Hook Station (South Western Trains)

Train service: from Waterloo, half-hourly Monday to Saturday; hourly on Sundays

Journey times (minimum): to Winchfield 40 miles, 53 minutes; from Hook 42½ miles 57 minutes.

Ticket: Day Return to Hook (available for leaving train at Winchfield on outward journey)

Introduction

Basingstoke was once a pleasant country market town, situated some 40 miles to the south-west of London. In post war years it became designated as an overspill area for the Inner City areas of London and as a consequence it has now become a rather characterless area with office tower blocks at its centre and miles of seemingly endless suburbs.

The Basingstoke Canal ran from the wharf in the town's centre to the River Thames at Weybridge, thus providing a link to London and its docks. Looking for the wharf and its surroundings will be of no avail today for all trace has been removed in the interests of progress. It was many years before that, however, that the canal fell upon hard times. Competition from the London and South Western Railway followed by the age of tarmac which improved the turnpike road (latterly known as the A30) caused the waterway to be obsolescent. As this century passed the bed of the canal silted up, the locks became impassable and the roof of Greywell Tunnel, a three-quarter mile bore which traversed a watershed some 8 miles from Basingstoke Wharf, partially collapsed.

Greywell Tunnel and the Basingstoke Canal

Notwithstanding the fact that the railway and the turnpike road have now been augmented by a motorway, the story has a happy ending. A decade ago the bed of the canal was in many places completely dry and in other localities resembled an overgrown ditch but there was a resurrection. Teams of volunteers cleared the watercourse, repaired the locks and in present times navigation for pleasure craft is viable right from Weybridge in the east to a point just short of Greywell Tunnel in the west. Repairs to the collapsed tunnel would be a major and expensive exercise and from the western portal of the tunnel to Old Basing on the outskirts of Basingstoke the course of the canal continues to be derelict.

The walk starts at Winchfield Station and the banks of the canal are reached after traversing a couple of miles. Then follows a delightful 3 mile stretch of tow-path passing under a series of restored bridges to a point of the southern outskirts of Odiham (which according to an early cycling tourist guide is equivocally described as a large village or a small town). With the appendage of an RAF station in the close vicinity the latter designation is now more appropriate. To see this still-pleasant country town with its wide High Street would need a diversion of about a mile by keeping straight on instead of turning right at the letter box after passing (or visiting) the Water Witch public house at Colt Hill.

The canal is rejoined at the village of North Warnborough and for just under one mile the final quiet stretch of the waterway is followed passing a drawbridge (over which passes a tiny lane) and then a quiet pool where the waterway widens out for a few yards, the latter being the utmost limit of navigation. The course now becomes a haven of peace and solitude as it winds its weed strewn way to the portal of Greywell Tunnel. Here the horses used to be detached from the barges, and walked over the hill to the western end of the three-quarter mile bore while the boatmen used to propel the craft by lying on the deck and using a technique known as "legging". Forward motion was generated by those responsible lying down and kicking the sides and the roof of the tunnel.

As described in the text of the walk, there is no shortage of licensed houses, one at the start at Winchfield Station, at Colt Hill, North Warnborough and Greywell on the route; and a choice of several in the Hook area. Also for those who do deviate into Odiham Town there are several pleasant establishments thereabouts to obtain refreshment. The terrain is just slightly undulating with nothing in the way of any extensive hill climbs. This part of Hampshire, only a few miles from its border with Berkshire to the north, is well wooded with lush pastures around the tiny River Whitewater which intersects with the canal (and provides some of its water supply) between the drawbridge at North Warnborough and Greywell.

Hook was until comparatively recently a smallish village where the road from Reading to Alton and the South coast met the A30 but of late the locality has become the centre of a rash of housing developments, and an industrial estate. These "improvements" are no doubt due to the fast train services available to London and the juxtaposition of the M3 motorway. The journey from Waterloo takes 50-60 minutes and a Cheap Day return ticket to Hook is of course available for leaving the train at the preceding station Winchfield.

The total distance of the walk is some 7¾ miles and nett of any stops the walk can be comfortably covered in 2¾ – 3 hours.

The Journey

For details from Waterloo to Pirbright Junction, see Route 1. Onwards from this point the main line continues through the pine woods of the Surrey Heath district and shortly one passes through a brick arch (one of a series of four each carrying a single railway track). This is an aqueduct over which flows the Basingstoke Canal, the immediate locality being known as Deepcut on account of the cuttings through which both the canal and railway run.

Soon one emerges from the wooded country and after passing the flat meadows and water-filled gravel pits which are features of this part of the valley of the Blackwater River. Then follows the spacious conurbation of Farnborough (of aircraft fame) and Fleet with its large tree lined pond visible on the left just before reaching the station. Three miles further on is Winchfield, the starting point of the walk.

The Walk

Leaving Winchfield Station by the main exit (on the "up" side), turn left along a road and continue slightly uphill to a T-junction where you turn left again over the railway bridge. After about a half a mile, turn left off this road at a wooden public footpath sign. Go forward for just a few yards and then left over a stile and onwards down the right-hand side of a meadow with woods on the right. At the end of this meadow, do not go through the gap ahead, but turn right over a stile and then on for a few yards over another stile, and down the left-hand margin of another field – i.e. with the hedge on the left. Where the hedge ends continue by crossing a ditch and forward, with the ditch on the right with a house visible ahead. On reaching the perimeter of the garden of this house, turn left with the garden on your right and then through a squeezer stile which leads out into a minor road.

The route lies ahead on this minor road for approximately one hundred yards, and then by a letter box, keep forward along a rough drive to Winchfield church, and through the churchyard with the church on the left-hand side.

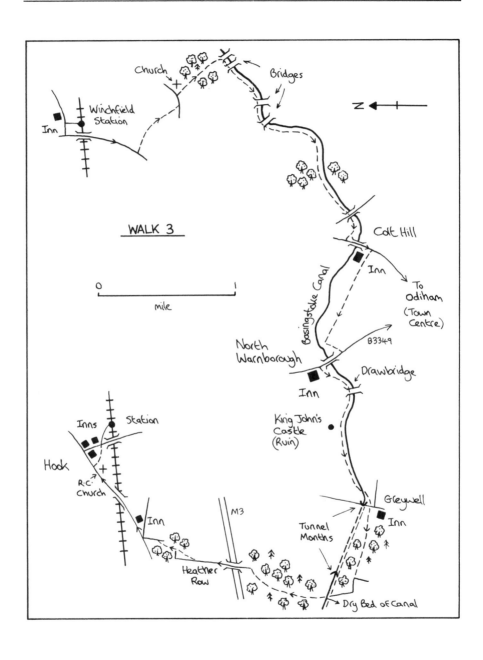

At the end of the churchyard, and slightly hidden by some bushes is a swing gate. Go through this gate and continue ahead along the right-hand side of the next field and so over a stile and into a wood. Shortly, you cross over two more stiles close together. The path continues clearly ahead through this lovely Hampshire woodland, which must be a joy to walk through at any season of the year. When the path eventually emerges from this wood, cross over a stile and continue clearly straight ahead across a meadow with the brick abutments of a bridge visible ahead. Do not cross this bridge, but turn left down a bank on to a towing path and then turn right under the bridge continuing on with the water on the left. This is the Basingstoke Canal, much of which has recently been reopened for navigation by pleasure craft.

The route then continues for approximately two miles along the towing path, passing under bridges known as Bratts Hatch Bridge, Sandy Hill Bridge, Broad Oak Bridge and then under an unnamed bridge under the Odiham by-pass road. A few yards after this un-named bridge is Colt Hill Bridge. Do not go under this bridge, but go forward up the ramp, and turn left over the bridge, passing a public house called the Water Witch, which serves a variety of good real ales and food. You are now at the southern edge of the small town (or large village) of Odiham. Having passed the public house, go forward along the road and up a rise. At a letter box, turn right, down a track and over a stile and forward across the middle of a large meadow soon picking up the line of a ditch on your left. Keep ahead with the ditch on your left, and then, approaching a wooded area, move gently to the right thus reaching the top edge of the meadow keeping the wooded ground on your left. At the top right-hand corner of this meadow, cross a stile which leads to a clear path ahead with the hedge continuing on the right. Ignore a crossing path and continue over yet another stile with the hedge still on your right and then over one further stile into some rough ground which leads after a few yards into a small track where, turn left with a small caravan site on your left. At this point the Basingstoke Canal is once again adjacent through the hedge on your immediate right.

You are now entering the village of North Warnborough. Cross the canal at the road bridge ahead and after crossing the bridge turn right down the ramp to the towing path and then right again under the bridge, resuming the journey along the towing path. After passing a "lift bridge", and having traversed a further quarter of a mile, you will see on the right the remains of King John's Castle. This was built by King John as a stopping place to rest and hunt while on his journeys from Windsor to Winchester.

After passing the Castle, and traversing a further short half mile, you come to the eastern portal of Greywell Tunnel. The path bears left over the tunnel and after a few paces emerges into a road where you turn right. Ten yards ahead is a T-junction where you turn right again. (Those requiring refreshment should go left for a few yards to a delightful village inn, the Fox and Goose). After about 30 yards turn left on to a footpath through a gap by a gate and go on under an umbrella of trees and hedges. Ignore a footpath which emerges from the left and continue uphill on what has now become a track. Eventually after rising further this track emerges into a meadow. (Ignore a stile on the left and go straight in to the meadow). Then go forward slightly diagonally to the right passing a solitary tree at a distance of some 30 yards on your left. A further solitary tree is now seen ahead. Pass this tree just to the left-hand side of it and go forward slightly downhill to the far left-hand corner of the wooded ground which is seen some 40 yards ahead. On entering the woods go left through a gap and after a few yards through a hand gate following a clear path going downhill, shortly crossing a track where again continue straight ahead.

The path now widens becoming a bridle way. This soon narrows again and becomes a hedged track running along the left-hand side of the woods. Continue along this clear path or track and after about a mile ignoring a gap in the fencing ahead (i.e. keeping just inside the wooded ground) emerging shortly at a quiet country lane where keep ahead with a large house on your right. Turn right where the lane bears right, (ignoring an enclosed path ahead). This tarred road soon becomes a rough track and after about 80 yards emerges at a recently refurbished bridge over what remains of the Basingstoke Canal. Pass over the bridge and continue straight on, the track now becoming rather sunken. Follow this track for a good half mile to a point where the motorway is on your immediate left (if the track is too wet or muddy, a viable footpath runs parallel on the left-hand side). The track now tarred rises for about 200 yards. At the top of the rise turn left across a substantial bridge over the motorway. Continue forward along the quiet lane which after a short quarter of a mile emerges on a green. There are a few houses here and just after passing the last house on the left, fork half right across the green as directed by a finger post and into some woods ahead. Follow the path which continues almost straight ahead through woods ignoring all tracks to the left and the right.

Signs of habitation will soon be seen ahead and the path eventually joins a rather gritty track which soon leads out into the main road at the Dorchester Arms, which appropriately enough sells good beer from Dorset and a good selection of pub food. Cross the first main road and pass the pub on your right and then join another road (the old way from London to Lands End, relieved now of much of its traffic on the adjacent motorway) and continue for a good three-quarters of a mile. Shortly after passing a Roman Catholic church on the right and at a bend where the road bends slightly to the right turn right into an enclosed tarred path with a "no cycling" sign. This will lead straight through to the station. If however, you require refreshment, you should ignore this path and continue for some 50 yards ahead to the village where there are two public houses on the main road.

Route 4: A Chiltern Traditional

Distance: 6 miles

Map: OS Landranger 165

Start: Great Missenden Station (Chiltern Line)

Finish: Wendover Station (Chiltern Line)

Train service (from Marylebone*): half-hourly (hourly on Sundays)

Return Train service (to Marylebone*): half-hourly (hourly on Sundays)
On Sundays depart from London (Baker Street) Station, changing at Amersham

Journey time (minimum): to Great Missenden 28¼ miles, 42 minutes; from Wendover 33¼ miles, 48 minutes

Ticket: Day return to Wendover (available for leaving train at Great Missenden on outward journey)

Introduction

The Chiltern Hills lie to the north-west side of the "London Basin" and form an arc some 60 miles long from their south-west extremity by the Thames at Goring in Oxfordshire (See Route 10) to the rather bare ridges that abound on the borders of Hertfordshire and Cambridgeshire in the vicinity of the towns of Royston and Baldock, some 40 miles to the north of London. The district in the main consists of chalky or flint subsoil and consequently many of the valleys contain no river bed, the rainfall permeating the soil and running underground.

There are exceptions, main being the Rivers Lea (or Lee), Colne, Gade, Misbourne and Wye which rise in the hills and form tributaries of the Thames. The area has proved very popular with walkers right from the beginning of "hiking" as it was known in the twenties and thirties, and indeed one of the very first books of country walks was published by the Metropolitan Railway Company in the 1920's. The villages around the railway stations became popular dormitory areas for London's business community and up to the outbreak of the Second World War; from stations such as Wendover and Amersham, etc, it was possible in the peak hours for commuters (who could afford first class fares plus a small surcharge) to travel right through to the City by a Pullman car which was attached to the otherwise suburban-like rolling stock.

The end of the Metropolitan Line: Amersham station with a 'Met' train in the reversing siding

The Chiltern Hills abound in beech woods but they do not monopolise the flora. The district also contains areas of dense coniferous woods and around the hilltop villages are often found areas of common land consisting of bracken, broom and ferns. In choosing the route for this traditional walk, I have selected an area of wooded hilltops and remote villages, all at an altitude of some 400 feet above the starting and finishing points of Great Missenden and Wendover. One will encounter very little through traffic in these hamlets and one is always far away from the noise of the motorways which, sad to say, penetrate some parts of the Chiltern area.

The distance covered is in the region of 6 miles and, apart from a fairly gentle climb from Great Missenden to the "heights" of Potter Row hamlet, and a few dips across the dry valleys, there is nothing sensational in the way of hill climbing. Indeed it is towards the end of the walk where a really steep section is encountered and this is in the form of a sharp descent from the 750 foot contour line near the tiny hamlet of Kingsash down through the woods to join the rutted Hogtrough Lane at an altitude of about 300 feet. This last ridge is of geographical importance in that it represents a watershed. As mentioned earlier the small rivers which rise in the hills flow southwards to the Thames. Here on the Wendover side the streams which gather in the vicinity of the town, flow northwards into the Midland Ouse and eventually wind their way through East Anglia and out into the North Sea at The Wash (which divides the counties of Norfolk and Lincolnshire).

So far as refreshment is concerned, there are pleasant taverns in Great Missenden itself at the start of the walk. Mention is thereafter made in the text of the three public houses en route, and finally at the destination of Wendover there is a variety of inns, cafes, and restaurants. The rail journey from London to Great Missenden involves about 40-50 minutes and day return tickets to Wendover are valid for leaving the train at Great Missenden.

The Journey

Marylebone was the last of London's great terminal stations to be built. It originally served the Great Central Railway with through express trains to Manchester, Sheffield and other cities in The North. Of more recent years the routes have been truncated and Marylebone is now London's "gateway" to the Chiltern Lines with trains traversing The Chiltern Hills to Bicester and Banbury others to Aylesbury, some continuing from Banbury to Birmingham.

On leaving Marylebone one enters a rather lengthy tunnel section taking the line beneath the hallowed turf of Lords Cricket Ground and the salubrious inner suburb of St John's Wood. The route emerges into daylight at Finchley Road from where it runs parallel to the

Metropolitan Line of London's Underground. At Neasden, some four miles on, the two arms of the Chiltern Line diverge. Shortly afterwards on the left-hand side will be seen the ornate Wembley Stadium, home of the football Cup Final since 1923. A few minutes later on the same side are the playing fields of Harrow School and on the hill above, the School itself and adjacent church.

After passing through Harrow-on-the Hill station the Chiltern Line shares tracks with London Underground's Metropolitan Line. There follows a series of refined and verdant suburban areas dominated by the one time country villages of Pinner and Northwood. It was the Metropolitan Railway who were mainly responsible for the transformation of this part of Middlesex into the commuter belt of today, hence the name of "Metroland" being applied in the 1930s to the locality. The railway built new or "refurbished" stations and the land was sold to builders, the train service enhanced and so over a matter of a few years an area of almost 100 square miles stretching from Wembley to Uxbridge and Northwood was changed from that of a mainly dairy farming landscape to that of a series of garden suburbs.

After passing through Northwood and Northwood Hills stations (stopping places only for the Metropolitan trains) the line passes through Moor Park (of golfing fame) and thence over the pastoral lands of the River Colne valley and the adjacent Grand Union Canal, and so into Rickmansworth, beyond which the climb into the Chiltern Hills starts. Wooded country gives way to common lands at the next station, Chorley Wood, followed by more (mainly beech) woods and green valleys on the way forward to Chalfont and Latimer, and Amersham.

Amersham Station is on a hill some 200 feet above the old town which lies in the valley of the Misbourne River (which is just a small stream). The picturesque High Street of (old) Amersham has changed but little in living memory. The district around the station itself (being known as Amersham-on-the-Hill) has a suburban character about it and apart from being a starting point for many Chiltern footpath walks is of little interest. On leaving Amersham, the line descends for the next four miles to the valley of the Misbourne River. (On this descent and from the left-hand side are glorious views of the valley including a glimpse of Shardeloes House, a mansion set in parkland on the opposite side of the Misbourne). After crossing the main Aylesbury Road the line passes by the tiny village of Little Missenden (not sufficiently populated to warrant a railway station but worthy of a by-pass road to steer traffic away) and so after 2 more miles in the Misbourne valley, to Great Missenden.

The Walk

Leaving Great Missenden Station from the "up" side go forward for a few yards by some shops into the High Street, then turn right and almost immediately left as signposted to Amersham, London and Chesham. About 150 yards ahead just by a sign indicating "two roundabouts ahead", turn left on to a footpath keeping straight ahead across a meadow and over two more stiles close together and out into the Great Missenden by-pass road.

Cross this main road (with great care) to a stile opposite and after crossing this stile, immediately turn left over another stile and proceed diagonally across a field rising uphill to a stile which is clearly seen ahead. Then diagonally across the next field to another stile at a gap in the hedge, and then onward continuing (still diagonally) across a third field at the end of which you cross yet another stile. Here keep forward on the right-hand side of this field with some wooded ground on your right. Where the boundary of the field on the right veers to the right, keep straight ahead for about thirty yards to a stile which is clearly visible ahead.

Cross this stile and proceed along the middle of the next field, through a large gap in the hedge and onwards across the next field with the hedge on your left. Continue along this clear path with a white water tower ahead. At the last gap in the hedge before the water tower, do not go through this gap, but turn left into the next field where you turn immediately right keeping to the right-hand side of this field (passing the water tower on your right) emerging into another field by another stile and keeping forward on the right-hand side. Then over yet one more stile out into a small road at Potter Row.

On emerging at this road turn right and continue for about 150 yards. Immediately after passing a dwelling named Hedgesparrow

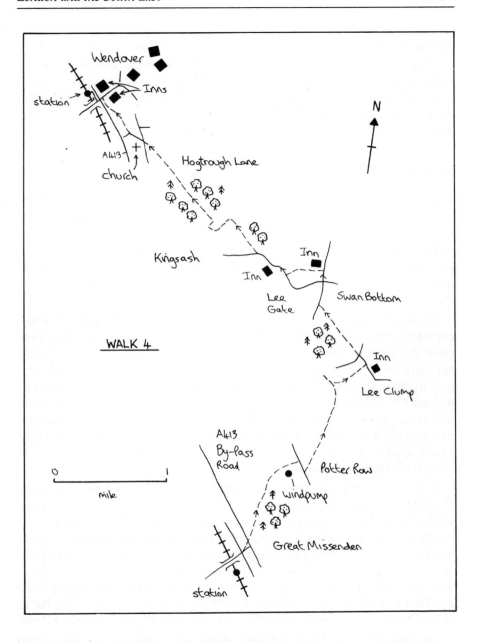

Wendover

Inns

station

A413

church

Hogtrough Lane

Kingsash

Inn

Lee Gate

Inn

Swan Bottom

WALK 4

Inn

Lee Clump

N

A413
By-Pass
Road

Potter Row

windpump

0   1

mile

Great Missenden

station

House on the left, turn left through a gate and then diagonally left across this field to a stile which can be seen about two hundred yards ahead. This stile actually turns out to be a double stile, across an old trackway. Having negotiated these two stiles keep straight ahead across the middle of the field in the same direction and on to a further stile in the far corner in this field. Continue onward across the next field passing an electricity pole just on your right. This path leads clearly on to a further stile visible at the end of this field. Continue straight across the next field and down to a dip by a hedge. At the hedge turn half right and follow the hedge round (with the hedge on your left) up to a further gate and stile, and out and forward into a small hedged lane.

After passing a house called Field End Grange, just a few yards onwards turn right (along a partly tarred lane) and after a few paces, where the hedge ends on the left, turn left going slightly downhill on a clear path to a stile which is clearly visible in the hedge in a dip below. Cross this stile, and turn right along a clear track. When the track ends, go over a stile and straight ahead uphill across another field with the houses of the village of Lee Clump ahead. Emerge from this field at a gate and stile with a house on your left and some barns on your right. Cross this stile and forward along a by-road into the village of Lee Clump. Here turn left at the main road. (Those in need of refreshment will see a few yards to the right The Bugle public house, which at the time of publication is not always open for midday sessions during weekdays).

Continuing along the road, one shortly reaches a T-junction where keep forward along a footpath with a hedge on the left and house gardens on the right, and forward over a stile and then ahead across a field firstly with a wire fence on the right. Where the wire fence bends to the right go only slightly to the right to a stile (or gap) at the right-hand corner of the field. Proceed along the right-hand side of some woods (which at the time of publication appear to be in the course of being partially felled). This track leads absolutely straight on ahead through the woods and out into a small road where you turn to the right. (At this point across the road is a feature of interest, in that a footpath goes right through the back garden of a house – note the two stiles). The occupants of the house have politely asked people to walk around the perimeter of the fence! Having turned right along the lane this soon leads to a crossroads in a dip at Swan Bottom. Here go straight ahead slightly uphill shortly arriving at the Old Swan public house which serves good food and real ale.

The Old Swan Inn at Swan Bottom

Just before passing this pub turn left along a rough gravel track and after passing a few houses on the left, go left (diagonally) on a footpath which crosses a field, at the end of which quite literally "duck" under a hedge (there is no stile), and continue in the same line (diagonally) across to the far left-hand corner of this large field and out into a small track which after a few yards emerges into a road at Lee Gate. Bear right in this road. On the left is The Gate public house which also serves good ale and food.

Continue up the road past The Gate and after about a quarter of a mile (where the road bends to the left), you will see on the right in the hedge a few steps leading up to a stile. Go up these steps and across the stile and diagonally across the field to the far corner at which point there is a belt of woods on the right-hand side. Cross a stile and go forward with the woods on your immediate right and so on following the right-hand perimeter of this field, eventually bearing left and left again and then right. At this point there is a stile on your immediate right. Cross this stile by the front of a house and straight ahead to a further stile at which point a clear path leads ahead going slightly downhill.

This path soon enters a wood, where keep straight ahead, steeply downhill now with just (currently) a small diversion round a fallen tree. Eventually on the left you will see a sunken lane. Follow the course of the path into this lane emerging at a junction of paths with a signpost on the right indicating the Ridgeway Path. At this point, keep straight ahead into a rough track (Hogtrough Lane) which follow for almost a mile.

Eventually you come out to a junction of roads where keep forward along Church Lane. After about a quarter of a mile, with a church on the left, and opposite a lych gate, turn right along a path and after about forty yards turn left through a gap in a wire fence and on to a concrete path across a recreation ground, then across a small tarred lane and through a kissing gate and diagonally left across the cricket ground out into London Road, Wendover. Here turn right and then left at a T-junction and a few yards ahead on the right is Wendover Station.

Route 5: The Kent and Surrey Borders

Distance: 7¼miles

Map: OS Pathfinder 187

Start: Edenbridge Town Station (Network South Central)

Finish: Oxted Station (Network South Central)

Train service : Half-hourly (Hourly on Sundays) – change at Oxted for Edenbridge Town

Journey time (minimum): to Edenbridge Town 25 miles, 48 minutes; from Oxted 20½miles, 36 minutes

Ticket: Day return to Edenbridge Town (Available for return from Oxted)

Introduction

Running some 20 miles south of London and more or less parallel to the Thames Estuary is the chalky ridge of hills known as the North Downs. A few miles south of this are the oddly named Greensand Hills consisting of a yellow sandstone. Beyond these ridges and north of the Wealden Hills is a quiet land of meadows and coppices, largely undeveloped except in the immediate vicinity of the towns of Edenbridge and Oxted etc where the inevitable growth has accrued, these being commuter towns for the workers of London.

This route of some 7¼ miles traverses meadowland and wooded areas with just gentle ascents and descents, the highest point of the ramble being no more than 100 feet above the lowest. But the terrain is nowhere flat. Little hillocks abound in all directions and never more than a few miles away are the high and steep escarpments of the North Downs and the wooded summits of the Greensands.

The town of Edenbridge consists in the main of one long very straight street, formerly one of the Roman roads that radiated from London to the vicinity of the south Coast. It boasts two railway stations, Edenbridge Town (which is where the walk starts) and Edenbridge North at a locality known as Marlpit Hill and close to the northern extremity of the town. The former station is on an old main route from London to Eastbourne but the line has been truncated at Uckfield leaving passengers for the seaside resort to deviate via Haywards Heath and Lewes. The north station is on a cross country line which links the Channel ports and East Kent with the west, via Reading. Although this link line contains some of the largest stretches of straight track in the United Kingdom it does not rate as a "high speed" connection mainly on account of the fact that through traffic has to reverse its direction at neighbouring Redhill.

Oxted is a product of the commuting era. Its shopping street is typical of the thirties and the adjoining avenues savour of prosperity. It nestles in a valley dominated by the massive Chalk Pit Hill to the north, and a gap in the Greensand Ridge immediately to its south. Although not a picturesque town it must offer a haven of rest for those whose daily labours involve a trip to London and in peak hours alternative services link the area both to London Bridge (for the City) and Victoria (for Whitehall and the West End).

As would be expected of a town of Edenbridge's size, there are facilities in abundance for refreshments at the starting point. The High Street has a variety of pleasant inns, cafes and take-aways. En route, a slight diversion leads to The Royal Oak public house some $3\frac{1}{2}$ miles from the start. Further on, the Hay Cutters inn is highly recommended. This lies some 2 miles from the finish, at which apart from some pleasant restaurants and a friendly cafe in a bakers shop, facilities are lacking, and possibly at times on Sunday afternoons may be non-existent. If such a situation should arise those in urgent need of sustenance may contemplate a break of journey at East Croydon which has spacious buffet accommodation on all platforms.

The total distance is in the region of $7\frac{1}{4}$ miles and a non-stop walk would take $2\frac{1}{2}$ to 3 hours at a leisurely pace. Cheap day return tickets to Edenbridge are available for return from Oxted.

The Journey

Leaving London (Victoria) station, one soon passes over the Thames at Grosvenor Bridge, with the high chimneys of the Battersea Power Station on the left. A minute or two later, one passes through Clapham Junction Station, self styled as the busiest railway station in the world. The way then passes through the somewhat sombre commons of Wandsworth and Tooting Bec. After passing Norbury Station there are views on the left of the South London Heights at the top of which used to be the glass building of the old Crystal Palace which was destroyed by fire in the 1930's. All that remains now of this long gone landmark is a television tower which stands on the site of the old Palace.

The tower blocks of the commercial centre of Croydon soon loom ahead and having passed through East Croydon one soon leaves the Brighton main line and diverts to the left into the Surrey Downs. At Riddlestown, there is a short tunnel under a spur of the downs, then on the right-hand side is the Caterham Valley along which runs the old main road from London to Eastbourne. On the left there are some magnificent wooded hills. It is hard to believe at this point, that one is only four miles from the centre of industrial and commercial Croydon. After passing Upper Warlingham Station the scenery becomes more rural and beyond Worldingham, a long tunnel is traversed under an area known as Chalk Pit Hill. At the middle of this tunnel the railway is some 500 feet below ground level which at this particular point attains a height of more than 800 feet above sea level.

On emerging from the tunnel, and on the left-hand side will be seen the vast chalk pit which has given its name to this particular hill and which is such a prominent feature of the North Downs. Arriving at Oxted it is usually necessary to change into the Shuttle train which runs from Oxted to Uckfield in Sussex. Another short tunnel (Limpsfield Tunnel) is traversed. This tunnel is through the Greensand Hills which at this particular point are not very wide. Following a stop at Hurst Green Station, pastoral country is traversed for a few miles, before another short tunnel. This short tunnel actually consists of two tunnels. In the middle of the tunnel, the line passes underneath another railway which is in a deep cutting. The tunnel is just broken for a few yards, thus explaining the flash of daylight as the tunnel is traversed. This can be viewed at close hand if during the walk on arriving at Little Browns, you take the first turning on the right to a railway bridge and then just to the right will be seen this most unusual and indeed unique piece of railway topography. Thence into Edenbridge Town station.

Unusual railway Topography at Little Browns. The Oxted-Uckfield branch is a tunnel, broken briefly by the intersection of the newly-electrified Tonbridge to Redhill line.

The Walk

Emerging from the "up" side of Edenbridge Town Station, proceed forward for about 200 yards to the main street of the town. Here turn left and after a few yards turn right along a road which is signposted amongst other things to the golf course. At a T-junction ahead, turn right as signposted to the golf course. After approximately half a mile and at the top of a slight rise, with a row of terraced cottages on the right, turn left along a rough track. After about 150 yards turn right over a stile and forward along a grassy track with farm buildings and

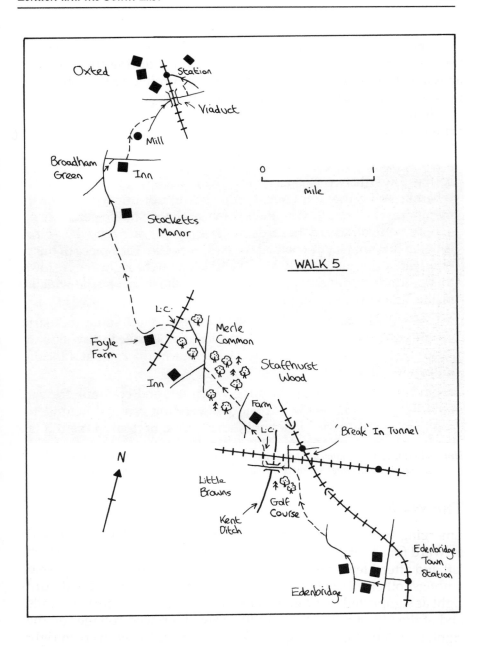

Oxted

Station

Viaduct

Mill

Broadham
Green

Inn

Stacketts
Manor

0 _____ mile

WALK 5

L.C.

Merle
Common

Staffhurst
Wood

Foyle
Farm

Inn

Farm

L.C.

'Break' In Tunnel

N

Little
Browns

Golf
Course

Kent
Ditch

Edenbridge
Town
Station

Edenbridge

stables on the left. Edenbridge golf course is on your right. After about 200 yards you will see a pond on your left where keep forward slightly right with a green of one of the holes on the right, and so slightly downhill to a small clump of trees on your right-hand side.

Finding a right of way across a golf course is never easy, except in those rare occasions where the walk is marked with waymarks. There are no waymarks here! Having passed the small clump of trees, and a small pond just behind them, bear slightly right across the golf course towards two isolated trees which are now ahead. Obviously when crossing the golf course, you should not impede any of the members who are enjoying their game, and you should certainly not expose yourself to any hazards by crossing the fairway when a ball is being driven! Having passed the two trees, aim for a piece of bushy or wooded ground slightly ahead and keep on the right-hand side of this ground; from here, proceed a little to the left to a stile which is visible in a wire fence ahead.

Cross this stile and go forward to a gate with some industrial ground ahead. At this gate, turn left over another stile into woods and so along a clear path which soon leads out into a road at a locality known as Little Browns.

On reaching this secondary road turn left and continue forward ignoring a turning on the right and descending gently downhill, the road being known as Honeypot Lane. At the bottom of the hill is a bridge over a little stream. This is the Kent Ditch which forms the County boundary between Kent and Surrey. Immediately past the bridge turn right along a signposted footpath, across a meadow, over a stile and up a ladder to the railway line. Be sure to stop look and listen, as the notice beseeches you to do. Descend the stairs beyond the railway and in the ensuing meadow, turn half left keeping in view some farm buildings immediately ahead. At the far corner of the field go through a gate and so along a clear track with the farm buildings on your right, through another two gates and into a minor road. Here turn right passing the gates of Partridge Farm and Black Robins Farm. the walks continues along this minor road for a short quarter of a mile and after the road has bent to the right (and where the road straightens out again) turn left along a clear woodland track. Ignore the first path on your left, but shortly afterwards where the clear track turns right, bear left along another track, which is just on the inside of the wood and then slightly downhill to a valley with a small pond visible on the left.

Just before reaching the pond, bear right and follow a small but distinct path keeping the pond on your left and proceeding forwards with the bottom of a little valley still on your left. Shortly there is a junction of six paths, and at this point go half left upon a small path through the woodland which soon leads into a secondary road. This beautiful woodland is known as Staffhurst Wood. Turn right in this road and continue for a short way to a road junction (on the left here at a distance of about a quarter of a mile is the Royal Oak public house which serves good and adequate food and drink and is a nice place for a halfway snack and rest). Those who are not going to the pub should proceed for approximately 100 yards and then fork left along a road which is signposted to Hurst Green and Merle Common. This quiet road soon descends through beautiful woodland.

The pinewoods of Merle Common

At a point where you reach a house on the left, do not pass this house, but turn left on a track which descends with the house on the right. This track shortly ends at a gate. Go through this gate and half right across the field to a hedge where there is a stile which is almost hidden by foliage. Cross this stile and forward across a further meadow to a level crossing over another railway (this is the line from London Victoria to East Grinstead, which will eventually be linked at East Grinstead with the privately owned Bluebell Railway). Having crossed the line (and duly stopped, looked and listened), keep forward over a further meadow to join a farm road (this is Foyle Farm). Keep forward between the farm houses and buildings. Eventually, this farm road bends sharply to the right and then to the left crossing a small stream.

Immediately after crossing the stream turn right through a large iron gate and proceed forward (and slightly uphill) to a gate and stile ahead. Continue over this stile with a hedge and ditch on your right and then over a set of two stiles with glorious views of both the Greensand Hills and North Downs of Surrey ahead.

Continue across the middle of the field over a small plank bridge and straight across the next field to a stile clearly visible about 80 yards ahead. Having crossed this stile a small stream has to be negotiated by means of a stone bridge across an old sluice.

From here, go ahead across another field with the hedge on your right. Where the hedge bends away sharply to the right, keep forward across the middle of this very large field, and so to the far hedge where veer right and so on to a minor road. The house ahead on the right is known as Spockett's Manor with its own oast house adjacent. At the T-junction ahead turn right as signposted to Oxted etc. passing Spockett's Manor on you right. Continue along this secondary road for a good three-quarters of a mile to Fordham Green.

At the beginning of the green, and just before passing a telephone box on the left, keep right along the greensward of this village green, by its right-hand boundary, emerging soon into another road with a pleasant hostelry the Hay Cutters Inn, immediately ahead.

Opposite the Inn is a stile and a footpath sign. Go across this stile and proceed along a very clear path and over three more stiles and so into an enclosed drive which soon leads into a small road by a mill.

Bear right across the mill stream, and immediately turn left along a footpath which diagonally crosses the first field. Cross either of the two stiles ahead and follow a clear path keeping a watery ditch immediately on your left, eventually crossing another stile and a little footbridge and into an enclosed track which soon leads out into a tarred drive which in turn leads into a road. Follow this road on to the impressive Oxted railway viaduct. Having passed under the viaduct, about 20 yards ahead is a steep alley where you turn left. This leads into a local road. At a grassy triangle ahead, bear right out into a road with shops, where you turn left and straight ahead to Oxted Station for the return journey.

Route 6: The Test Valley

Distance: 7½miles

Map: OS Landranger 185

Start: Overton Station (South Western Trains)

Finish: Whitchurch/Hants Station (South Western Trains)

Train service: from Waterloo, every 2 hours

Journey times (minimum): to Overton 55½miles, 54 minutes; from Whitchurch 59 miles, 59 minutes

Ticket: Day return to Whitchurch (available for leaving train at Overton on outward journey)

Introduction

The upper valley of the River Test is in the extreme north of the county of Hampshire, the river subsequently turning southwards eventually going out in to the sea at Southampton Water. This easy 7½ mile walk is from the town of Overton to Whitchurch, and traverses some of the quietest stretches of the whole river.

There are opportunities for refreshment shortly after the beginning of the walk in the town centre of Overton, after which there are no further facilities until the end of the walk apart from the excellent Watership Down Inn, at Laverstock. At the end of the walk there are abundant facilities in the town of Whitchurch, including a delightful tea room serving all sorts of snacks and which is situated in one of the few silk mills left in the country.

The River Test is a trout stream, and these fish and many others can usually be seen in the clear waters. The going is quite easy, and there is nothing in the way of any hill climbing, and indeed without an intermediate stop at Laverstock the journey can be comfortably covered in a matter of three hours. Some six miles north of the walk is the hill known as the Watership Down, this being at a point where the county of Hampshire borders on the county of Berkshire. Many readers will be familiar both with the book and the television series of the antics which took place in this somewhat remote location. Day return tickets to Overton are of course available for alighting at Whitchurch on the outward journey.

Whitchurch station, with a train from Waterloo to the unlikely destination of Tisbury, deep in the heart of the Wiltshire countryside. The platforms have recently been extended to accommodate 9 car trains

The Journey

For the journey as far as Winchfield station, please see the texts to walks 1 and 3. Beyond Winchfield, the railway keeps in an absolutely dead straight line for approximately nine miles to the town of Basingstoke. This town used to be a rural market town, but in the post war era, it became one of the satellite towns of London, and now has endless suburbs, mainly of council houses stretching up to four miles from the original town centre, very little of which now remains. After leaving Basingstoke, the walk becomes distinctly rural again, and on

approaching Overton, the views to the south will include a valley in
which is the spring which is the source of the River Test.

The Walk

Leaving the down side of Overton Station, turn right along a lane with
some industrial buildings on the right and after about 200 yards
where the industrial buildings end turn left down another lane,
Copps Road. After a further 250 yards where the lane bends to the
left go forward through some wooded ground and continuing downhill along a clear path ignoring another which leads to the left. After
about a quarter of a mile the path emerges in a road where keep
straight ahead for a half a mile to the town centre of Overton. (Just
after passing the fine parish church on the right there is a slightly
humped bridge across a ditch and about 100 yards further on across
another bridge one gets ones first glimpse of the River Test itself, here
quite a narrow stream running through the back of the town). Cross
over the town centre cross roads with the White Hart on the left (open
all day and also serves coffee in the mornings), and proceed ahead
along Winchester Street.

At the Greyhound pub about a quarter of a mile ahead turn right
along Greyhound Lane passing straight over a cross roads, the continuing road now being known as Dellands. After passing a row of
old cottages on the left and where the road bends right, keep forward
on a track. After about 300 yards at a junction of tracks turn left. After
about a mile the gravelly track bears to the left and at this point keep
straight ahead along a grassy path between fields. This is in fact the
continuation of the same track, which has obviously in recent years
been diverted to the left as a more convenient outlet to the nearest
road. This is one of those ancient trackways which abound in this area
and nearby Pilgrims Farm seems to indicate its southern direction
towards Winchester Cathedral. The path gradually ascends to an arm
of the Hampshire Downs known as White Hill.

Ascending and passing over the brow of the hill the track continues
straight forward with a hedge on the left and through a wooden five
bar gate and so forward with a wire fence on the right. Ahead is a belt

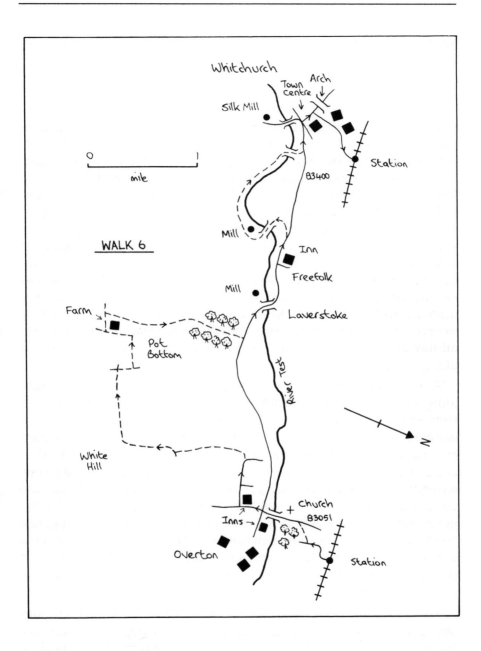

of trees on the left and a further plantation of trees on the right. Immediately before the trees on the right turn right through an iron gate and continue ahead through a dip along a clear track. After passing through the dip the track leads straight ahead with the hedge on the right and so forward over a stile (with a gap to the left of it if still available) continuing ahead along the line of some electricity poles. Eventually there is a hedge ahead and at this point follow the track round to the right with the hedge continuing on the left. After about 100 yards turn sharp left along another track with a hedge to the left. The track eventually bears left at quaintly named Pot Bottom Cottage where keep ahead with the buildings of Laverstoke Grange Farm ahead.

Pass the main farmhouse building on the right and then immediately turn right between the farmhouse and other farm buildings on to a tarred farm road. After about 100 yards and just beyond the last of the farm buildings on the left turn right on another track, with a footpath signpost, which leads clearly ahead winding to the left through a dip and then slightly to the right as it ascends the far side of the dip. Here is a T-Junction of tracks and the way ahead is by way of a footpath which runs to the left of a belt of trees. On breasting the top of the rise there are views ahead of the Test Valley and the clear path continues with the narrow band of trees on the right through yet another dip (not quite such a deep one this time) and so to the corner of the field into some woods from where the path leads clearly ahead and slightly downhill and then more steeply through a plantation.

At this stage one is quickly descending to the Test Valley itself. With wire fencing on the right the path soon leads out into the main road at Laverstoke, where you turn left. (At one time this used to be the main A30 highway from London to Lands End but some 30 years ago the route of this was diverted over to Salisbury Plain through Sutton Scotney and Stockbridge). Laverstoke Mill is on the right. This mill until comparatively recent times used to supply the paper on which money was printed.

You soon reach the next village, Freefolk, the entry to which is made over a hump backed bridge across The Test which, since last encountered in Overton, has gained in size and strength. On the right after passing the river is a very attractive group of thatched houses. At the end of the village and for those who require refreshment, just round a corner, on a turning on the right, is the Watership Down Inn. Excellent ales and a good variety of food are available here.

Thatched cottages and wishing well at Freefolk

For those not making this small diversion to the Inn, continue straight along the main road for a short half mile follow the left-hand pavement of the road and at a point where a row of fairly modern houses on the right ends fork left, alongside a footpath sign and onwards to a tree enshrouded path with views of the River Test through the undergrowth on the left. After a short half mile this path emerges into a tarred lane where you turn left. This lane soon leads to a humped backed bridge once again over the Test where follow the tarred drive round to the right towards a mill. Before the gate into the mill fork left upon a grassy track which leads slightly uphill with a wooden fence on the left. This soon leads to a gate and stile where continue forward into a meadow with the hedge on your right. After a good half mile keep forward over another stile with the hedge continuing on your right and with some hilly ground on the left. From here, go over another stile and ahead in the same direction. You are now back alongside the river which can be seen through the hedge on the right.

Eventually, where a school building looms on the left, there is a junction of paths and at this point turn right over a picturesque footbridge (again over the River Test) with Town Mill on the left and so along a tarred drive (with more of the river Test on your right) shortly emerging into the main road where you turn left. Three hundred yards forward is the town centre of Whitchurch. At the main crossroads (it is in fact a junction of five roads) ignore the extreme right-hand turn, Newbury Street, and go half-right along Bell Street. At the cross roads some 200 yards ahead, and shortly before reaching an archway, take the right-hand turning as signposted to Whitchurch station which is just over a quarter of a mile ahead, on your left.

Route 7: "Where the Waters End" – Radlett to Brookmans Park

Distance: 7¾miles

Map: OS Landranger 166

Start: Radlett Station (Thameslink)

Finish: Brookmans Park or Welham Green Stations (Great Northern)

Train service: from Kings Cross, Thameslink every 15 minutes (half-hourly on Sundays); from Welham Green* or Brookmans Park* every half hour (hourly on Sunday)
On weekdays change at Finsbury Park for Kings Cross

Journey times (minimum): Kings Cross Thameslink to Radlett 13½miles, 20 minutes; from Welham Green to Kings Cross 15½ miles, 40 minutes; from Brookmans Park 14½miles 38 minutes

Tickets: Kings Cross Thameslink to Radlett: single (outward); from Welham Green or Brookmans Park to Kings Cross: single (inward)

Introduction

To the north side of the Metropolis and beyond the northern termini of London Underground at Barnet, Edgware and Cockfosters the suburban sprawl quickly gives way to a comparatively thinly populated and pastoral area. The change from the endless chain of suburbs to the peaceful countryside of South Hertfordshire is really quite abrupt.

This walk (which is the only one of three in the book which is partly inside the ring of the M25 motorway) takes in some of the quietest countryside within a 20 mile orbit of London. The ground is well wooded and undulating – the highest point of the walk being more than 200 feet above the lowest. At the beginning of the journey there are ample facilities for refreshments in the village of Radlett, the High Street abounding with cafes, restaurants, and public houses. Places of refreshment along the route are described in the itinerary, but alas, a pleasant public house, The Wagon and Horses at Ridge Hill has recently disappeared in the name of progress having been replaced by the M25 motorway. Regarding refreshments at the very end of the journey, there is a matter of 100 yards over the railway bridge at Brookmans Park, The Brookmans Park Hotel which has restaurant facilities and bars with good ales, the locality itself being a high class garden suburb type of development built in the thirties for the benefit of commuters to The City.

And so we come to the reason for the title of this route. The Mimmshall Brook does not like any other normal river or stream, find its way into a larger stream or river and thence out to the sea. In the rather swampy meadows behind the village of Water End the Mimmshall Brook and other small tributary streams quite literally disappear down holes. Geographers call this sort of place (which is very rare indeed in the United Kingdom) a "depression". At Water End the land all around rises slightly, and consequently the streams and rivers that gather there have no natural outlet through a valley and have to pursue thereafter a subterranean course. It is possible after a very dry spell to go closely up to the point where the water disappears, but normally this is a somewhat treacherous exercise because in view of the nature of the terrain, the ground around the swallow holes is apt to be very marshy and swampy.

The total distance of the walk is some $7^3/_4$ miles, and with reasonable conditions, and without stopping *en route* can be leisurely covered in a matter of $2^1/_2$ to 3 hours. As the outward and inward journeys are by different routes single tickets will need to be purchased.

The Journey

Kings Cross Thameslink station is a somewhat subterranean structure with its entrance in Pentonville Road, some 150 yards to the east of the main line building. This is the monopoly of the Thameslink line which runs from Brighton in the south, and Bedford in the north. If more convenient the journey could start at the preceding stations of Farringdon, Blackfriars, London Bridge, or City Thameslink, but not the latter on a Sunday.

Leaving Kings Cross Thameslink it is about 1 mile before the line emerges in daylight with a shorter tunnel to follow before Kentish Town station .. in a rather drab area sandwiched between The West End and the hills of Hampstead. The latter are subsequently pierced by 2 tunnels, the longer of which burrows under the hilly suburb of Haverstock Hill. Daylight again and onwards through suburban areas of West Hampstead (some 200 feet in altitude below the heath), Cricklewood, Hendon and Mill Hill. At the latter views ahead herald an emergence into more rural landscapes, and indeed to the east of Mill Hill Broadway station (NW7) there is a surprisingly attractive belt of country stretching to Totteridge Village (N20) some 3 miles away, certainly the quietest portion of The London Postal District by far.

With the busy M1 motorway on the right vistas of green fields open up on the opposite side. Passing under the M1. a hilly ridge is traversed by the half mile long Scratchwood Tunnel which is followed by Elstree and Borehamwood station which is actually in Boreham Wood itself as indeed were the famous British Film studios. Elstree village itself is an attractive hilltop village some three-quarters of a mile south-west of the station. One of the reasons for the rural nature of this part of Hertfordshire so close to London is that a projected extension of the London Underground Northern Line from Edgware never materialised. Building on this project commenced in 1939, was suspended on the outlook of World War 2 and never resumed. Indeed in some fields north of Edgware there are remains of an unfinished viaduct, reminiscent of an abandoned railway, but uniquely a railway that never was!

The Return Journey

This is given for this particular route because an entirely separate line is encountered. Brookmans Park station lies at the western extremity of a salubrious dormitory suburb of the 20th century. Rural surroundings abound (except in the immediate vicinity of Potters Bar Station) right through to New Barnet where suburbia is re-entered. Between Potters Bar and New Barnet is the somewhat isolated station of Hadley Wood, sandwiched between two tunnels and adjacent to a hilly ridge known as Enfield Chase. A series of suburban stations follow with Finsbury Park the final halt if the train is going on to Kings Cross (Main Lane) as would be the case at week-ends and Bank Holidays. On this route some three-quarters of a mile from Finsbury Park and on the left-hand side is Highbury Stadium, home of Arsenal Football Club since they moved from Woolwich in the early part of the century.

Alternatively, if the return journey is made on a week day there is little or nothing to be seen as the line uses a former underground railway tunnel terminating at Moorgate in the heart of the City of London.

The Walk

Leave the station on the "down" side, turn left through the station yard up a flight of steps at the top of which turn left over the railway bridge. Continue on this road, (Shenley Hill) and at the top of the hill at a crossroads turn left along The Avenue. After about 200 yards fork right along another quiet road, The Warren. Where this road bends to the left go through a wooden gap along a path which leads firstly downhill and then uphill through some wooded ground. Follow this clear trackway through the woods ignoring any minor paths to the left or right. The edge of the woods is on your left, and a golf course to the right. You will eventually emerge through a gap in the hedge at the far left-hand corner of the wooded area.

Ahead is a hedge. Keep to the left-hand side of this hedge, and after about three hundred yards, go through a gap in the hedge and down a cart track which clearly leads forward into a drive. Ignore the left-hand turn (a tarmac drive through some hospital grounds), and continue slightly right and ahead. A few yards on, the main gravel drive turns off to the right and at this point keep forward along a lesser track which rises gently uphill and so through the middle of a field

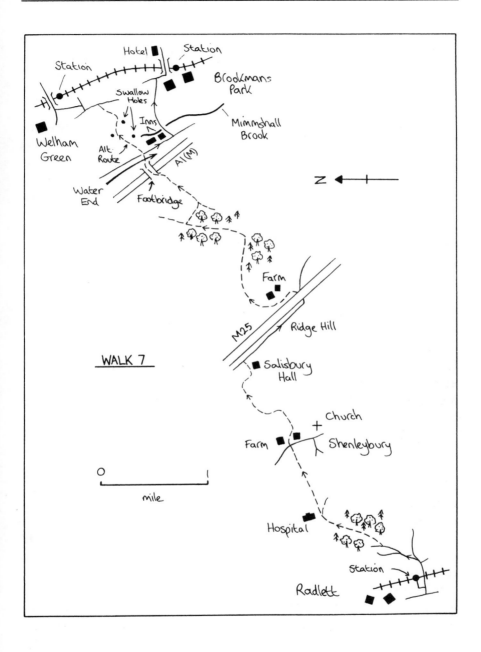

Station

Hotel

Station

Brookmans Park

Station

Swallow Holes

Inns

Mimmshall Brook

Welham Green

Alt. Route

A1(M)

N

Water End

Footbridge

Farm

M25

Ridge Hill

WALK 7

Salisbury Hall

Church

Farm

Shenleybury

0

mile

Hospital

Station

Radlett

with a wooded area ahead. Keep this wooded area on your right and continue along the middle of the same field with the houses of the hamlet of Shenleybury ahead. (About a mile to the left will be seen the ribbon of traffic circumnavigating the London area by means of the M25 motorway).

Ignoring all branches the clear track eventually veers slightly to the left and emerges at a secondary road at the northern end of the hamlet of Shenleybury. Cross this road to a signposted bridleway opposite through farm buildings. The (concrete) track veers right and then left and continues as a bridleway between hedges eventually turning sharp left and shortly on bending to the right to pursue its original course. The bridleway now assumes the character of a green lane and emerges through avenues with sports grounds to the left and right. Continuing to ignore paths to the right and left, the way eventually emerges amongst buildings where follow the main way, right for a few yards and then left and forward along a tarred lane for some 200 yards to join another secondary road with the M25 towering above immediately behind.

Here turn right and continue for a mile over the summit of Ridge Hill and downhill to a point where the road burrows under the M25 at a bridge. Immediately after passing under the bridge turn left up a concrete drive which shortly bears right and then to the left in between a farmhouse and a silo. Having passed these features turn right and follow a clear track between fences. Where the track peters out, go half right through a gate keeping the woods immediately on your right. At the far right-hand corner of this small field go ahead between posts which mark the old right of way. Then turn right for a few yards and then left with a ditch on your right and proceed gently downhill all the way to a gravel drive. Turn left here, and so slightly uphill and on through woods. At a point where the woods on the right eventually end, turn right over a stile by the gate and continue forward at the right-hand side of the meadow with the woods continuing on your right and over a further stile, and then through the middle of another field down to a track. Turn left here and continue straight ahead for a short half mile to the main A1/M Motorway ahead.

Here turn left with the motorway on your right and shortly cross this by a footbridge over the motorway which leads into the hamlet of Water End. Cross over the first road and turn right along the second, Warrengate Road, as signposted to Brookmans Park. Shortly on your left you will pass The Woodman Inn an excellent free house serving beer and food. A few yards on you pass another inn with similar credentials. Neither establishments currently serve food on Sundays! A short distance on take a left-hand turn signposted to Brookmans Park. After a few paces this crosses a bridge over the Mimmshall Brook. (It is approximately a half a mile on the left that this brook and others quite literally disappear in holes with no visible outlet to any other river or the sea). Continue along this road to a T-junction where you turn right with Brookmans Park Station ahead.

The Woodman – one of the two congenial inns at Water End

Alternative Finish

For a closer inspection of the ground where the rivers and streams disappear turn left after negotiating the footbridge over the motorway. After a few yards, turn right over a stile and follow the grassy path through a bushy area. Shortly on the right is a densely vegetated depression in which the waters of the Mimmshall Brook and its tributary stream The Catherine Bourne meet their visible demise. As mentioned in the introduction to this route this ground is treacherous with swamps and swallow holes. Keep to the clear path eventually crossing a footbridge and continue along the left-hand side of a field with more swamp ground to the left. Eventually cross another footbridge. The stream below has no direction of flow being close to its point of disappearance. (Wooden guideposts along the way show the path as leading to Welham Green). The clear path continues with wooded ground to the right and after a short while leaves the border of the wooded area and continues clearly ahead and out into a small road. Here turn left, first right first left and in a quarter of a mile right again for Welham Green Station for trains back to Kings Cross.

Route 8: To The Town of Thame

Distance: 7 miles

Map: OS Landranger 165

Start & Finish: Haddenham and Thame Parkway (Chiltern Line)

Train service: from Marylebone, hourly (2 hourly on Sundays)

Journey time (minimum): 41¾miles, 52 minutes

Ticket: Day return to Haddenham and Thame Parkway

Introduction

The town of Thame is a pleasant place and its High Street has not changed very much in appearance since the beginning of the century. To the north of the town centre lies the River Thame, a tributary of the Thames which it joins at the Oxfordshire village of Dorchester (not to be confused with the better-known and similarly-named county town of Dorset.)

Like most rural towns it is not without its blemishes. On the route of the walk one passes a small industrial estate which lies well outside the town, but this is something of a one-off situation, because before entering the area and after passing through it, the landscape is pastoral. There is another industrial estate south of the town in the neighbourhood of the old railway station. Indeed, Thame did have a railway until comparatively recent times: it was on the most direct line from London to Oxford branching off from the old Birmingham main line at Princes Risborough and re-joining the present main line to Oxford at Littlemore junction, just south of Oxford City.

The beginning of the route is at a comparatively new station called Haddenham and Thame Parkway. This new venture has served to partly rectify the inconvenience caused by the closure of the old Thame and Haddenham stations, which were in fact on two different lines.

The neighbourhood of Thame which is on the fringes of the Vale of Aylesbury is still extremely rural. Although the general locality is described as a vale, it is not flat, and indeed some of the villages north of Thame are on hills which rise up to 250 or more feet above the river valley. In the background and to the south-east direction is the mighty escarpment of the Chiltern Hills which rise in this particular locality to 800 feet above sea level, some 500 feet above the level of the vale.

The parish church of Thame with the cricket pitch in the foreground

The walk itself does not present any hill climbs whatsoever. Just a few gentle undulations upon entering and leaving the valley of the sleepy river. Refreshments can be obtained at Haddenham (see the end of the text of the route for the locality of these establishments). There are of course abundant facilities for all types of refreshment in the town of Thame, whether one's choice is a pub, cafe, hotel or restaurant.

The total length of the walk is approximately 7 miles, and the circular tour can comfortably be covered in a matter of 2¾ hours. Haddenham, the starting and finishing point is a pleasant old Buckinghamshire village, but during the past few years (and particularly since the opening of the new station), has something of a suburban sprawl to the north-west of the old village. There is a story about this village which may be apocryphal: the inhabitants of the village were so fond of their livestock, that they erected a roof above the duck pond to keep the ducks dry when it rained!

The Journey

For the journey from London (Marylebone) to Beaconsfield, see route 11. Leaving Beaconsfield a descent of some $6\frac{1}{4}$ miles ensues, firstly on a high embankment, followed by a short tunnel. Thereafter the line emerges above the valley at the River Wye, not the Wye that forms the boundary between England and Wales, but a smallish stream which rises in the neighbourhood of West Wycombe and runs into the Thames at Bourne End. Alas! The Wye Valley at Wycombe is a ribbon of industry. Timbers from the surrounding woods made the area a hive of the furniture industry, a narrow ribbon albeit as wooded hills abound to the north and south. Leaving High Wycombe station (one of those peculiar instances where the platforms are staggered – i.e. the up and down sides do not face each other but follow in sequence), the valley route becomes more residential and after 2 miles one nears the picturesque village of West Wycombe dominated by a tower surmounted by a golden ball to be seen on left-hand side on the top of a steep hillside. There are caves below which have in recent years been commercially exploited. There are legends that the tower and adjacent church had associations with the Dashwood family and the "Hell Fire Club".

The route now becomes wholly rural, with views of the village of Bradenham with its triangular village green and Bradenham House, once home of the Victorian statesman, Disraeli. Saunderton station follows next, some 3 miles from the village after which it is named. A descent from the Chiltern ridge follows with a peculiar feature of the up and down lines taking separate courses (thus making the gradient easier for ascending trains) and so into Princes Risborough, gateway to the Vale of Aylesbury, which the poet Rupert Brooke described when viewed from a neighbouring hilltop as "The Slumbering Midland Plain".

The remaining few miles are through agricultural country, and the railway has been reduced to a single line, quite a demotion from its not too distant status as the main line from London to Birmingham, Chester and Birkenhead.

The Walk

Leaving Haddenham and Thame Parkway station by the exit join a road and turn right for about 250 yards to a crossroads where again turn right into a tarred lane which eventually emerges after a short half mile into the main Aylesbury-Thame Road. On joining this road turn left. Ignore a private drive signposted to Notley Abbey and about 150 yards further on, just after a sign indicating there are parking facilities in a quarter of a mile, turn right (as directed by a public footpath sign) and so slightly downhill across a field. At the end of this field ignore the rough track on the right and keep straight ahead with the hedge on the right leaving this next field via a stile where keep half left eventually coming out at a footbridge. This is the River Thame which joins the (River) Isis at Dorchester on Thames and so becomes the "Thame-Isis" i.e. what we know as the Thames.

Cross this bridge and bear left. The path leads forward along something of a causeway with a further arm of the River Thame on one's right. After about 150 yards turn right crossing this other arm of the river by a bridge and proceed forward for about 30 years to a stile on the left of an iron gate. Cross this stile and immediately turn sharp left into a field. As you cross this field move gradually to the right away from some wooded ground and emerge at the far right-hand corner of the field where there are two stiles. Ignore the stile on the right and take the stile on the left (i.e. in the far corner of the field). Go forward and cross a stone footbridge over a small brook. Continue ahead in the next field with the hedge immediately on your right and bear right where the hedge bears right. On reaching a "gap" do not go through the gap but turn very sharp left into a track (with the field that you were in continuing immediately on your left). At the end of

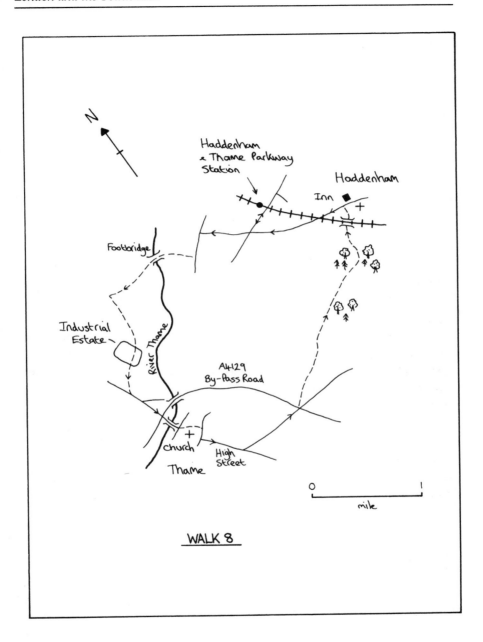

WALK 8

the field the track bears right, where continue straight ahead across another field soon joining a hedge on your left and with some industrial buildings ahead. This industrial area is entered by a stile at which point keep ahead between the buildings and through two gates which cross a carriageway. After this point there are industrial buildings only on the right-hand side, with an industrial yard on the left. On reaching the perimeter of this area turn right at the T-junction and after about fifteen yards turn left over a stile (which is preceded by a plank bridge) and then 10 yards ahead across another stile which crosses wire fencing and then half left across the field to a gate and stile clearly visible about 75 yards ahead. On passing this stile keep forward with the hedge on your right across two meadows (the second which rises slightly uphill) to join the main road into Thame where you turn left. (The spire of the parish church can be seen ahead and in the further distance the high escarpment of the Chiltern Hills in the neighbourhood of Kingston Blount and more to the right, Christmas Common).

Cross the road to the right-hand side pavement and where the main road bears left continue ahead along what was the old main road (before the by-pass road system was adopted here), eventually crossing another main road (more of the by-pass system) and continue with the spire of the parish church immediately in the front of you. Shortly the road becomes a causeway of bridges over various arms of the River Thame and on crossing the main river towards the end of the causeway one also crosses the county boundary between Buckinghamshire and Oxfordshire. On approaching the church go up a few steps into the churchyard and then turn left along an avenue of trees eventually leaving the churchyard via a kissing gate. The path continues straight ahead across the cricket ground to a further kissing gate at the far right-hand side, where you turn right along Bell Lane which winds its way first left and then right to a roundabout at the far west end of the spacious High Street where you turn right.

Continuing along the left-hand side of the pavement with the Town Hall and its Clock on the right. A short quarter of a mile after passing the town hall fork left along a road signposted to Princes Risborough and Aylesbury and continue for about three-quarters of a mile until you come to a roundabout. Cross over the road signposted to Oxford and Aylesbury and go ahead along a rough track with a rugby football ground on your left. This track keeps straight ahead and after about a half a mile becomes a field path leading straight across a large field to its bottom right-hand corner. At this point hidden in the foliage on the right is a stile. Cross this stile and bear left along the right-hand side of the green meadow passing through a small avenue of trees and through a large iron gate with a small house on the left.

A track follows but ignore this as it bends round to the right. Instead go ahead over a stile and into a large field. Continue over this field just skirting a small belt of trees (on your left) and at the top right-hand corner of this belt of trees go ahead aiming for the far left-hand corner of another belt of trees that lie about 400 yards ahead. Then continue ahead with the belt of trees immediately on your right. Having passed the trees proceed in the same direction eventually passing a farm-house on your right and so forward through an iron gate.

The way continues on to a point some three hundred yards ahead where there is some wooded ground on the left. There is not much to show of the path here but continue forward slightly bearing leftwards towards the wooded ground and then over a fence into the next field with the woods now immediately on your left. Some 40 yards further on turn left into the woods soon crossing over a substantial footbridge and on in to a tiny enclosed path which soon emerges at a stile into a meadow. Cross this meadow to a bridge under the railway which can be clearly seen about 400 yards ahead. Then cross a fence and proceed under the railway bridge and bear immediately to the left along a clear path that leads for about 20 yards to a substantial kissing gate. (The tower of Haddenham church is seen about 200 yards to the right). Continue along the clear enclosed path through another (again substantial) kissing gate and so on out into a small road at Haddenham Church End.

On emerging from the footpath turn left and at a T-junction ahead turn left again. For those needing immediate refreshment there are two excellent public houses just a few yards to the right. Having turned left, continue along the road which eventually crosses a railway bridge and after a further short half mile comes to a crossroads where you turn right to the railway station some 300 yards ahead.

Routes 9a and 9b: Surrey Commons

Route 9a: Some Surrey Commons

Distance: 3½miles

Map: OS Landranger 187

Start: Effingham Junction Station (South Western Trains)

Finish: Cobham Station (South Western Trains)

Train service: from Waterloo, half-hourly (hourly on Sundays)

Journey time (minimum): to Effingham Junction, 21½miles, 38 minutes; from Cobham 18 miles, 33 minutes

Ticket: Day return to Effingham Junction (Available for return from Cobham)

Route 9b: More Surrey Commons!

Distance: 6½ miles

Map: OS Landranger 176

Start & Finish: Esher Station (South Western Trains)

Train service: from Waterloo, half-hourly

Journey time (minimum): 14½miles, 24 minutes

Ticket: Day return to Esher

Introduction

These two routes are unique within this book in that they can be linked up to form longer routes. North East Surrey abounds in areas of commonlands. In Route 9a, five of these are traversed, and in 9b another six, making eleven in all, The start of Route 9a at Effingham Junction is about 2 miles from the village and there is no "Railway

Tavern" or any other place of refreshment in the vicinity. The only facility en route is the Cricketers pub at Downside Common which although having something of a limited range of real ales from the national breweries, it has a very wide range of food to suit all tastes. The tables at the front of the pub are pleasantly situated on the common itself and at a south-west aspect forming a delightful haven to enjoy sustenance on a fine day.

The tiny parish church at Downside Common with village pump in the left foreground. An elderly inhabitant told the author that the building was once used as a bakehouse!

The chain of commons often means that you pass from one to another with no distinct boundary. At other times the intervening land is occupied by very high class housing developments, the buildings in the main not obtruding on to the highways as they are set well back and shrouded by the trees of their front gardens. These "estates" were originally constructed in the 1930s for those who found good fortune at the end of their daily pilgrimages to the City of London. Nowadays it may be assumed that some occupants are blessed with the virtue of having been born in the oil rich lands of the Middle East, with a possible smattering of a few who have reaped a fair harvest through the medium of popular music.

And surprise, surprise! On Route 9a you will pass quite close to the Isle of Wight and on 9b to the Scilly Isles. The former owes its name to a clearing in the woods where a number of dwellings stand in the middle of Bookham Common. On a map where woodland is denoted by green shading, the "enclave" shows up a veritable white island. The Scilly Isles have a more subtle derivation. Kingston-Upon-Thames was one of the very first towns to benefit from a by-pass, and where this new road joined the old in the vicinity of Ditton Common, traffic islands were constructed is such a manner that to pursue the circumlocutory course demanded, cars had to proceed at a dead slow pace. The motorists of the day described them as silly islands, hence the present day title of the locality "The Scilly Isles".

The village duck pond at West End Common

The routes are mainly level with only slight undulations. Route 9b is similar save a gentle descent to West End Common and village, followed by a short sharp rise thereafter. The proximity of the River

Mole is the cause of the slight change in altitude. Much of the subsoil is sandy and quite drying, but areas of clay also abound where the going can get very tacky after a wet spell. Return tickets to Effingham Junction are available for return from Cobham, but if the routes 9a and 9b are combined to finish at Esher, single tickets should be purchased for the outward and inward sections.

The Journeys

Route 9a

For the journey as far as Surbiton, see route 1. Some 2 miles after passing Surbiton at what is known as Hampton Court Junction one leaves the main line to the left. At this somewhat sylvan locality of outer suburbia it is difficult to envisage that in the spring of 1945 a German V2 rocket landed causing heavy casualties and serious damage to the railway and surrounding property. No scars now remain or this wartime incident. The railway soon reaches Hinchley Wood station, adjacent to the Kingston By-pass where in the early thirties motorists used to frequent to picnic on the grass verges! This was a very early venture in the world of by-passes and formed part of the A3 London-Portsmouth road.

The line continues to Claygate passing through a landscape of sports grounds and agricultural scenery and then to Oxshott, set amidst the pines (and opulent properties) of Oxshott Heath. More extensive areas of sports fields abound around the next station, Cobham, which serves the localities of Church Cobham and Street Cobham as they were separately known until comparatively recent times. The village now known generally as Cobham is about 1½ miles away joined by a main road or a somewhat rural by-way which traverses a series of "greens" collectively known as Cobham Tilt. One soon arrives at Effingham Junction joining up with a longer route from London which goes via Croydon, Sutton, Epsom and Leatherhead.

Route 9b

For the Route 9b journey, see Route 1 from London (Waterloo) to Esher.

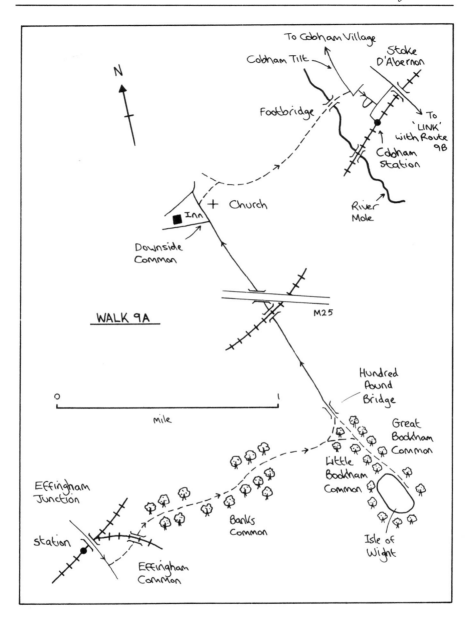

Walk 9a

From Effingham Junction station turn right on leaving. After about 50 yards by a bus stop turn left along a clear track. You are now on the first of the commons, Effingham Common. Soon after passing under a railway bridge the main track bears to the right. At this point keep ahead along a bridle path which goes straight ahead just inside the left-hand side of the wooded common area. After about half a mile you pass on to a second common, Banks Common. The way continues straight ahead with the thick bushes of the common on your right and open pastures on your left. Eventually there are woods on both sides of the track and ignoring the other tracks which emerge from the left, pass a few houses on your right. At this point go slightly left and straight ahead along a clear path which leads to the left of a National Trust signboard. Just *before* reaching this signboard turn left along a clear grassy path which winds its way through bushes and trees and then over a little footbridge emerging into a minor road. (This road as it enters The Common on the right forms the boundary between the two more commons Little Bookham and Great Bookham Common.)

At this point turn left along the minor road over a small bridge (Hundred Pound Bridge it is called) and follow the quiet by-way for a good 1¼ miles passing on the way under the railway and the M25 in quick succession. At a junction of roads a choice arises. If refreshment is required turn left on to Downside Common and after a quarter of a mile cross the "green" to The Cricketers public house which can clearly be seen from the road, returning after sustenance to the aforementioned road junction, where you turn left.

After a few yards and by a very tiny church turn right along a footpath which crosses a field and soon joins a private road (a public right of way) where you turn right. Shortly bear left where a private way to a farm veers to the right. The ensuing bridle way emerges after some half mile to cross a footbridge over the River Mole and on joining a residential road continue ahead for a few yards and then right on an enclosed path signposted to Cobham Station (which incidentally is in the village of Stoke D'Abernon, some 1½ miles from Cobham itself!). At the end of this path go straight ahead ignoring two turnings to the right and right at a T-junction into Cobham Station yard. This is the end of walk 9a but, if you wish to extend it by including walk 9b, you will need to add the following link:

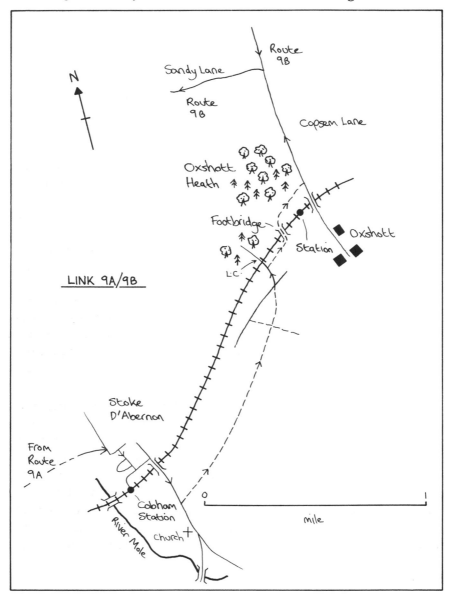

Link between Walks 9a & 9b

Distance: 2½miles

Map: OS Landranger 187

Start: Adjacent to Cobham Station

Finish: Junction of Copsem Lane and Sandy Lane (Oxshott Heath)

Instead of bearing right into Cobham station yard, turn left – soon emerging into the main road where you turn right, soon crossing a bridge over the railway. A quarter of a mile after the bridge, just before reaching a house on the left called The Old Rectory turn left across a stile. Beginning as an enclosed path between hedges, the path shortly emerges at another stile where keep forward ignoring a track on the right and continuing up the right-hand side of a steadily rising field. After passing a house on the right the path continues straight ahead to a stile clearly visible at the skyline. Pass this and continue along the right-hand side of the next field and so over the brow of the hill continuing with the hedge on your right at the bottom of a steep rise. Then over another stile and continuing along this clear path with the hedge on your left and over yet another stile and a plank bridge to a point where there is some wooded ground on your left-hand side. This path soon emerges at a bridle road. Cross this bridle road to a footpath straight ahead, this clear path continuing and emerging after about a quarter of a mile into a secondary road where you turn right.

Shortly this secondary road bends to the right, and at this point keep ahead across a green patch into another road. It is in fact a continuation of the same road, Blundell Lane. Just before reaching a railway level crossing fork right along a footpath with the railway on the left. Shortly cross a footbridge and continue with the railway now on your right. Continue ahead past Oxshott Station and turn left at the main road to soon join the junction with Sandy Lane. Here the remainder of walk 9b can be joined to end at Esher Station, or if required to join the beginning of 9b at the turning to the station at the Cafe Rouge.

Walk 9b

Esher Station is about 1 mile away from Esher itself, situated, as it is, bordered on three sides by Ditton Common and on the south-west side by the expanses of the elegant Sandown Park race-course. Leave the station on the "down side" (main exit) and turn left with Ditton Common on the left and Sandown Park race-course on the right. At a T junction ahead (with The Cafe Rouge on the corner) cross the main road by the push-button traffic lights and continue ahead along a clear path into the trees and bushes of Littleworth Common. After about half a mile the path joins a rough track, keep straight ahead here through posts to a metalled road (Littleworth Road) which follow for about half a mile to a cross roads at Harelane Green. At the cross roads is situated the Swan Inn which can provide excellent sustenance for those needing such facilities early in the route. Continue straight across the cross roads into Arbrook Lane and follow to its end at the perimeter at Arbrook Common.

Here, on reaching the common, veer just to the right at a cottage and through posts. At a junction of paths some 20 yards ahead take the right-hand turn signposted "Horse Ride to Esher Common". Follow the track of hoofs and after about a quarter of a mile where hoof-marks diverge, take the right-hand fork and then a little further on a left fork and so out in to a tarred track where you turn left. In about 150 yards at a point where a path crosses the tarmac track turn right, soon emerging at a larger and cindered bridle way which leads after a few yards into Copsem Lane. This is nowadays a busy highway linking Esher and Leatherhead with the A3 trunk road. (If incidentally you should make any error in navigating the horse paths of Arbrook Common have no trepidation, for by keeping in the same south-westerly direction you will eventually emerge in Copsem Lane at some point hereabouts).

Turn right on reaching this main road and follow for about three-quarters of a mile passing *en route* the roundabout and underpass below the A3. At a road junction ahead turn right along a by-road (Sandy Lane). After about half a mile the lane emerges from the wooded areas and enters a locality of elegant houses which abound in this area. Just after having breasted the top of a rise and on the right

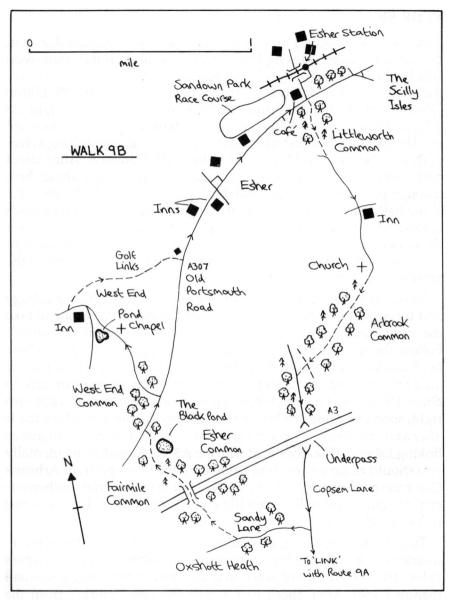

O |_____|
                    mile

Esher Station

Sandown Park
Race Course

The
Scilly
Isles

WALK 9B

Café   Littleworth
              Common

Esher

Inns   Inn

Golf   Church +
Links
        A307   Arbrook
West End Old   Common
        Portsmouth
Pond   Road
Inn + Chapel

West End
Common
              The
              Black Pond
                            A3
              Esher
              Common
                          Underpass
N
                        Copsem Lane
Fairmile
Common
                  Sandy
                  Lane
                              To 'LINK'
    Oxshott Heath   with Route 9A

by a house named Silver Greys turn right and follow an enclosed path which descends between fences. After about a quarter of a mile this path emerges on to common land. Ahead and on the right is Esher Common and to the left the extremities of Fairmile Common. The path soon emerges into a clearer path coming in from the right which some 200 yards ahead ascends to a bridge across the A3 road. (It is at this point that the enormous change that has taken place since the building of this road can be fully understood, the highway cutting a huge concrete swathe through some of the finest heath and common land in South-East England). Once over the bridge turn left as sign-posted to the "Portsmouth Road" and through a veritable cathedral of pine trees to a further guide post ahead where you turn right (again signposted to the Portsmouth Road) passing through some posts and ahead along a causeway.

The peaceful reed-strewn lake on the right is known as Black Pond. Having passed the pond, pass through some "posts" and then straight ahead at a junction of paths and tracks. Shortly the perimeter of the common is reached where bear left with a fence on your right and so in about 75 yards out into the (old) Portsmouth Road. In times gone by this used to be a busy trunk road. Nowadays it has been relieved of much of its traffic by means of the adjacent A3 and M25.

Cross the road to the pavement opposite and turn right. The common on the left is West End Common. After a short rise and subsequent descent turn left along a quiet by-road, West End Lane. This lane soon descends through trees to the peaceful backwater of West End. As you enter the village green there is a reedy pond on the left, followed by a spacious cricket ground and a larger pond flanked by willows. Note also the well-preserved Victorian corrugated iron chapel on the right. At the apex of the green is the Prince of Wales public house where in addition to good bar facilities there is also an adjacent restaurant.

Follow the road round a left-hand bend to a point some 50 yards ahead to a narrow enclosed path on the right which runs between the gardens of houses on a gently rising gradient. After a right-hand bend the gradient becomes steep and one emerges on to a golf course where the clear path runs straight ahead between the fairways. After passing the golf links the path becomes enclosed again and soon emerges on to (old) Portsmouth Road at the top of Esher High Street.

Follow the High Street gently downhill (passing the many inns and catering establishments of the village) for a full mile to the Cafe Rouge (if you did not notice it on the outgoing route, observe the splendid circular milestone outside the cafe). Some quarter of a mile ahead are the Scilly Isles! (See "Introduction" to the route). However, at the Dome Cafe turn left for Esher Station, retracing your steps of the outgoing journey for these 300 or so yards.

A Victorian 'Tin Chapel' at West End Common

Route 10: The Goring Gap

Distance: 7 miles

Map: OS Landranger 175

Start: Pangbourne Station (Thames Trains)

Finish: Goring and Streatley (Thames Trains)

Train service: from Paddington, half-hourly (hourly on Sundays)

Journey times (minimum): to Pangbourne 44¾ miles 39 minutes ; from Goring and Streatley 48½ miles, 56 minutes (both by fast train from Paddington, changing at Reading)

Ticket: Day return to Goring and Streatley (Available for leaving the train at Pangbourne on outward journey)

Introduction

The Thames, pursuing its course from the Cotswolds and down through the plains of Oxford, was confronted on the borders of Berkshire and Oxfordshire with a range of high hills which stretched from Wiltshire in the South-West to Bedfordshire in the North East. To make way for its tortuous journey down to the sea it had to find a way through this obstacle and did so by means of the Goring Gap, a valley between the Berkshire Downs and the Chiltern Hills.

When Brunel built his railway from London to Bristol this was an obvious route to take, being as it is only a gentle gradient from the county town of Reading to the Vale of White Horse which stretches for some 30 miles to the north of the downs. Before the railway came the turnpike road from Reading to Wallingford and Oxford, and now all three – railway, road and river – squeeze together through the narrowest part of the gap in the vicinity of Pangbourne, a village which is twinned with adjacent Whitchurch on the opposite bank, as indeed Goring is with Streatley.

At both of these points the river is bridged by minor roads and from the bridges are seen two of the most attractive weirs on the whole of the river. The sides of the valley are well wooded, particularly on the Oxfordshire bank and the walk will take the reader through some of these woodlands, eventually emerging some 2 miles before the finish at a point in a quiet by-lane where extensive views open up towards the Great Vale.

Taverns and Inns are a-plenty at Pangbourne or Whitchurch at the start and further opportunities occur *en route* at Crays Pond and Woodcote as described in the text. At the finish there are ample opportunities in the delightful inns at Goring (and over the bridge at Streatley). Favourites of mine are The Catherine Wheel or The John Barleycorn on the Goring side, but let this not detract from the many others including The Bull in the centre of Streatley and, for those who prefer to take refreshment closer to the railway station, there is the Queens Arms with its traditional Oxford ales.

Starting as it does in the Thames Valley and visiting the hill country one obviously will encounter an initial gradient and some "ups and downs" but at no place can the walk be described as strenuous. The total distance of about 7 miles (the last two of which are mainly downhill) can be traversed (non-stop) quite comfortably in 2½ – 3¼ hours. Day return tickets to Goring and Streatley are available for departure on the outward journey at Pangbourne, but be sure to give the full title if booking from a suburban station as there is another Goring on (what was) Network South-East by the Sussex Coast.

The Journey

It was the great Victorian engineer, Isambard Kingdom Brunel, who built the railway from London to Bristol and this journey traverses the first 40 or so miles of his route. Leaving London (Paddington) station – 'The Gateway to the West' – one encounters the usual prelude of inner urban scenery which, after a couple of miles, opens up on the left to the expanse known as Wormwood Scrubs. After passing the new international train depot of North Pole (named after a nearby pub) is seen on the far side of "The Scrubs" – the famous prison.

Thereafter follow Acton and Ealing, the latter (like Surbiton in Surrey) being styled early in the century as "The Queen of the Suburbs". Hereabouts, the surrounding terrain is mainly flat and unlike many of the railway routes that emanate from London termini, there are no deep cuttings or tunnels. However, just after passing West Ealing and Hanwell the fact that one has been gently rising is highlighted by the traversing of a viaduct over the valley of the River Brent which aptly enough flows southwards to join the Thames at Brentford.

The industrial outer suburbs of Southall, Hayes and West Drayton are soon left behind and just after the latter station the River Colne is crossed and the County of Buckinghamshire is entered. Soon one passes Slough followed for 3 or more miles (on the right-hand side) by its massive trading estate which grew up in the thirties and provided jobs for local people and many immigrants from South Wales during the trade recession of that era. Burnham follows next (with its famous Beeches some way to the north of the station) and then Taplow. Between here and Maidenhead the Thames is crossed and on both sides there are views of a pretty section of the river as one crosses into Berkshire. Beyond Maidenhead the view becomes more rural and almost 10 miles are traversed before the next station, Twyford. During this stretch there are views northwards of the southern extremities of the Chiltern Hills.

Since crossing the Thames at Maidenhead, one has been gradually rising; a descent through a deep cutting (Sonning Cutting) finds us rejoining the Thames at Reading, whose suburbs extend some 3 miles westward to Tilehurst where the railway is virtually on the banks of the Thames. The slopes of the Oxfordshire Chilterns are beyond. From here, a pleasant $3\frac{1}{2}$ miles takes you to the start of the route at Pangbourne where the little River Pang (or Pang Bourne) joins the mighty Thames after its short journey from its source deep in the Berkshire Downs.

The Walk

Leaving Pangbourne Station on the down side go through an alley which leads out into the main road where you turn right to the village centre. After about 200 yards turn left as signposted for the A329 to Reading, and after about another 50 yards, (after crossing a little bridge over the River Pang) turn left again, as signposted to Whitchurch. Proceed firstly under the railway and then over the River Thames into Whitchurch village. (The toll which is applicable to vehicles at this bridge does not apply to pedestrians).

Continue up the main street ignoring all turnings to the left and right (including a bridle way signposted to Goring). Eventually after a considerable uphill climb the road passes a war memorial on the left. Some 30 yards past this and where the road bends to the right continue ahead along a clear footpath which for about 20 yards rises considerably to a fork in the path, where keep left. After a few yards go over a stile and then along the left-hand side of a large field. At the end of this field go through a swing gate and proceed along a "cartway" which soon descends between hedges with the buildings of Beech Farm ahead.

Pass the farm buildings on your left going through a swing gate emerging after a few yards into a drive, which crosses diagonally to a further swing gate. Then cross a small field with wire fencing on the left to a further gate ahead which leads into some woods. A few yards into the woods the path forks slightly to the right and then winds round and continues on a course about 10 yards inside the right-hand boundary of the wooded ground. Eventually there is a further fork in the paths where take the right-hand path. This continues clearly on with the boundary of the woods now a little more over to the right, emerging at a clearing. Here the path becomes enclosed between wire fencing. After passing through this short clearing the path goes into wooded ground again leading after about 30 yards into a farm drive with outbuildings on the right and left. Continue ahead emerging soon at some gates into a minor road where you turn right.

After about 40 yards turn left through a gap in the hedge and on entering a field go diagonally to the left to a stile which is just visible in the hedge ahead.

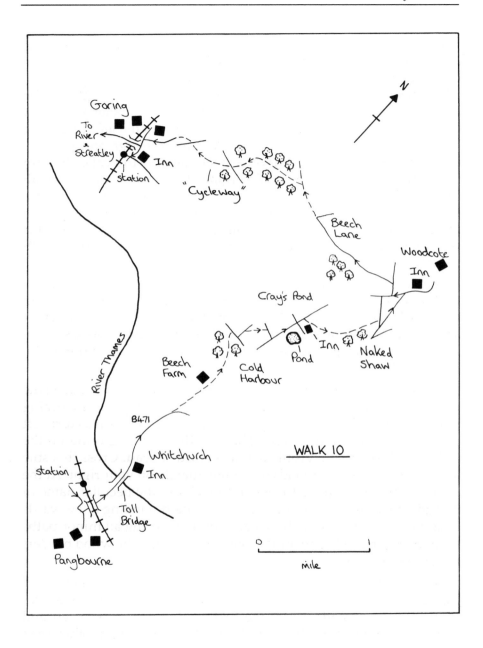

On crossing this stile the path veers slightly to the right where aim ahead using as a marker the roof of a house which is visible at the brow of the hill. The path emerges from the field via a stile just to the left of the house, into a small tarred road where you turn right. At the junction about 40 yards ahead turn left down a smaller road. Just before reaching a house called "The Cottage" (on the left) turn right over a stile which is somewhat hidden in the hedge and proceed diagonally left on a clear path which goes downhill to a valley bottom with a red brick house ahead. Emerging at a stile join another small road and bear right for about 200 yards to a T-junction and on to a secondary road where you turn left. Follow this for about a quarter of a mile to the cross roads at the village of Crays Pond. (The pond is seen on the right just before the cross roads and is now strewn with reeds).

Ahead is the substantial White Lion public house which serves traditional beer, hot and cold food and has a nice sunny south-facing beer garden. Immediately after passing the public house on the right and opposite a filling station on your left fork right across a stile by an iron gate and go forward with a hedge firstly on your right, followed then by some woods.

At a stile ahead bear slightly to the left across a field to another stile which is clearly seen to the left of some electricity poles. Emerging into a small road turn to the right and after just a few yards turn left over another stile and proceed ahead with wooded ground on the right to a further stile visible about 50 yards ahead. Cross this stile and continue with the woods now immediately on your right. At the next stile the path enters the wood (which has the peculiar name of Naked Shaw) where continue ahead, the path winding a few yards round to the left. Follow this clear path on ignoring all minor paths both the right and left eventually emerging where the wood borders the corner of a field.

At this point go forward to an enclosed path with wire fencing and the field on the left and the woods on the right. The path soon emerges at a junction of roads. Cross the first road and then bear left and continue forward for a half a mile eventually joining another road (where those requiring refreshment should bear right emerging after about 100 yards at the Red Lion public house at Woodcote village).

Those not requiring refreshment should turn sharp left as signposted to Whitchurch and Goring. After a short quarter of a mile turn right at a turning, Beech Lane, and after a further 200 yards at the foot of a dip turn left (where Beech Lane itself turns left). After about a half a mile the signs of habitation disappear and Beech Lane (still tarred) goes through a beech wood and then along the side of another on the left. Ahead on the right-hand side is a view of the Vale of White Horse.

Eventually where the tarred part of the track ends, continue straight ahead and down hill. At a point on the left where the woods begin, turn left up the bank and past a wooden post and on through a rather faint path which runs diagonally into the woods. After about 300 yards cross a "ride" and continue straight ahead (the path is still rather faint) but can be distinctly discerned keeping in the same line as it was before crossing the ride (although slight diversions may be needed to avoid fallen trees). Reaching a stile a clearer path is joined where you turn left for just a few paces and then right along an even clearer path. This continues in a downhill direction eventually bending left as it emerges from the woods with a wire fence now on your right and the steeply wooded hillside on your left. The path eventually becomes totally enclosed under an umbrella of hedges and shrubs and shortly emerges into a minor road where you turn right.

After a few yards turn left upon what is now described as a cycle-way. This turns out to be a path which runs slightly uphill with fencing on the right and then continuing downhill just inside the woods with glorious views of the Berkshire Downs ahead to the right. Eventually the path emerges from the wood by the remains of an old kissing gate and then over a stile. Here continue just inside the right-hand side of a field. The path veers slightly away from the right-hand side of the field climbing gently to a stile. Cross this stile and go forward into a track which after 30 yards leads into a minor road. Turn left in this minor road for just a few yards and then turn right and then immediately left through some fencing. The ensuing tarred path leads ahead and then bears to the right and enters an area of modern houses where keep straight ahead. Where this road (Lock-stile Way) eventually bends to the right, go straight forward through a passageway which soon leads into a tarred drive where continue forward (i.e. slightly right) for about 200 yards to a cross roads where you turn left* and head forward for about another 200 yards into the forecourt of Goring Station.

*For those wanting to see the river and the various attractive taverns in Goring and Streatley villages, keep straight across the railway bridge for about half a mile, to the river bridge by a weir, which leads across to the Berkshire village of Streatley. There is also a very attractive public house just outside the station, The Queens Arms, which serves a good selection of snacks and genuine Oxfordshire Beer.

A leafy track above Whitchurch-on-Thames

Route 11: Another Chiltern Traditional

Distance: 7¾miles

Map: OS Landranger 165 & 178

Start: Beaconsfield Station (Chiltern Line)

Finish: Amersham Station (Chiltern Line & London Underground)

Train service: from Marylebone half-hourly (hourly on Sunday); from Amersham half-hourly (On Sundays London Underground to Baker Street half-hourly)

Journey times (minimum): to Beaconsfield 23 miles, 29 minutes; from Amersham 23½miles, 36 minutes

Ticket: Single to Beaconsfield (outward); single to Marylebone or Baker Street on Sundays (inward)

Introduction

No excuse is made for a second visit to this delightful area other than to say that the region is so vast that an entire book could be written (as indeed many have been), of the extensive network of paths that abound herein. The route here is in a south-north direction starting from the "New Town" area of Beaconsfield. The old town and High Street, which are worth a visit lie about a mile south of the station. The modern area around the station consists of shops and (mostly opulent) house properties built in the commuter boom of the thirties.

Beech woods predominate in this locality and the landscape is one of riverless valleys interspersed with hills. the walk itself features a gentle rise for the first 3 odd miles to the hill top village of Penn perched on a ridge from which can be seen to the south, Windsor and its castle, when visibility permits. William Penn, the founder of Pennsylvania lived nearby and thus emanates the association of this Chiltern village to one of the great cities of the United States. After passing Penn there are ascents and descents to negotiate. The climb from the road junction at Penn Bottom through the woods towards

Penn Street is short but "formidable", in contrast to the gentle down-grade which follows a mile or so later from the hamlet of Mop End to the Misborne valley at the western extremity of Amersham.

At this point, one might find an exception to the aforementioned dry valleys for the Misbourne River sometimes flows after a wet season and if it is in this phase it pursues a pretty course through the town of Amersham itself. It is an unfortunate fact that nowadays the bed of this attractive stream is often dry, as is the case with some other watercourses of south-east England, particularly those which traverse or rise in areas of chalky soil. It has been said that if the Misbourne flows all year round it bears an ill omen, because it apparently did just that in the summers of 1914 and 1939 which were followed respectively by World Wars I and II.

The Crown at Penn

Apart from the beginning of the walk at Beaconsfield (New Town) facilities for refreshment, mostly in idyllic surroundings are quite numerous. You literally pass the back garden of the renowned Royal Standard of England at Forty Green. A mile and a quarter on, one is confronted by The Crown at Penn with surely one of the most attractive frontages of the many ancient inns in the Chiltern area. After another 1½ miles or so, are The Hit and Miss and The Squirrel, smaller than the previous establishments but also serving good ales and a variety of food in a friendly atmosphere. These inns are in the somewhat scattered village of Penn Street, not a street in the sense that one ordinarily assumes, but a separate village to Penn itself, with its own parish church and a really delightful village green upon which cricket matches are played during the season, to a backdrop of the mighty Penn Wood beyond the far boundary.

If one is not tempted to halt at Forty Green, Penn or Penn Street, there are abundant facilities for refreshment of all kinds in the pretty High Street at Amersham (old town), just three-quarters of a mile from the finish of the walk, a finish which incidentally involves a short sharp climb out of the Misbourne Valley to the heights of the New Town and the railway station. The total distance of the walk is about 7¾ miles, a matter of some 3 to 3½ hours steady walking if stops are excluded. On the outward journey from Marylebone station a single ticket to Beaconsfield should be purchased and on the return a similar ticket from Amersham to Marylebone. As the starting and finishing points are on different arms of the Chiltern Line, day return tickets are not available.

The Journey

For the beginning of the journey from Marylebone to Neasden Junction see Route 4. At Neasden the Wycombe Arm of the Chiltern Line forks off to the left shortly passing Wembley Stadium station, the stadium itself towering above the railway on the immediate right. Thereafter follows a spell through the Middlesex "garden suburbs" of Sudbury and Sudbury Hill and on via a short tunnel to Northolt Park, a dormitory area built on and around a horse race-course which thrived hereabouts prior to World War 2. Soon the line burrows under and joins the old Great Western Railway from Paddington at Northolt Junction (or South Ruislip as it is now known). It was through here until some 20 years ago that an hourly service of crack express trains operated from Paddington in London to Birmingham and Wolverhampton in the west Midlands. Some of these expresses continued on to Birkenhead (for Liverpool) including in this itinerary a brief incursion in and out of North Wales in the area south of Chester.

Nowadays the track is the monopoly of the Chiltern Line and on the left-hand side keeping it company is the western outpost of London Underground's Central Line which terminates alongside the Chiltern Line at West Ruislip. Hereafter, the scenery becomes rural as this corner of Middlesex is (compared to the remainder of the County) only sparsely populated. Some 2½ miles after leaving West Ruislip can be seen the remainder of a station formerly known as Harefield Road, closed now for over 70 years, probably due to the fact that Harefield Village was a good 2½ miles away.

A viaduct over the River Colne takes us out of Middlesex and into Buckinghamshire and to Denham (formerly of film studio fame) and Denham Golf Club, a small station which served local golfers before the days when most had the privilege of their own private (car) transport. Another viaduct soon follows, this one over the Misborne River, and shortly after a bridge spanning the ubiquitous M25 ring road. The railway is now climbing earnestly into the south-eastern slope of the Chiltern Hills soon reaching the salubrious neighbourhood of Gerrards Cross, which station also serves the nearby villages of Chalfont St Giles and Chalfont St Peter.

Next comes Seer Green, the station for the Quaker village of Jordans and for Beaconsfield Golf Club. As was the case at Denham, few golfers now arrive by rail and use the direct exit from the down platform to the clubhouse. A couple of miles of rural scenery take one on to the destination at Beaconsfield.

The Walk

Leave Beaconsfield Station by the down exit and proceed up the "ramp" and then turn right across the railway bridge. At the roundabout a few yards ahead fork left along Reynolds Road, keeping on the right-hand side pavement. After about 100 yards the road bears to the left, and at this point continue straight ahead along a tarred footpath which after about 30 yards enters a track where bear left.

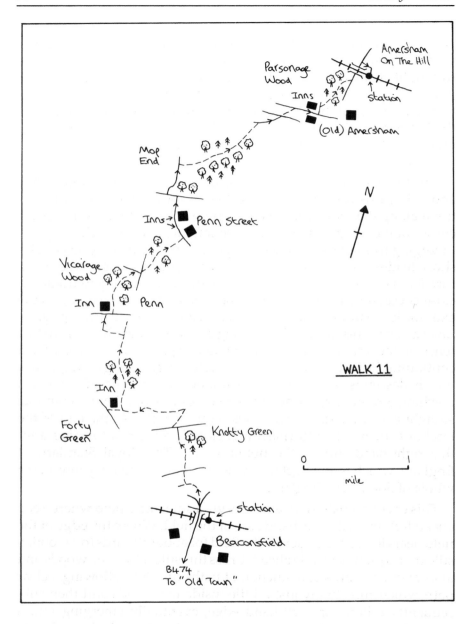

After a short quarter of a mile at a junction of tracks turn right (along what is the most used of the two tracks) and then after a few paces fork right again along an enclosed path which runs between wooden fences. Cross a road and continue straight ahead (the path continues to be enclosed). At the point where the fencing on the right ends take the left-hand fork of the two paths with a wooden fence continuing on your left and so out into a quiet residential road which follow in a forward direction.

Shortly this road emerges at a T-junction where you turn left. After about 30 yards turn right into a gate into some allotments and continue along the path with a hedge on your left. At the far left-hand corner of the allotment grounds turn left into a small enclosed path. Emerging from this short enclosed path go forward along an equally short dead-end drive and through a swing gate into a field where you turn left. Follow the left-hand corner of the field crossing two stiles in close succession and shortly a further one and so on (keeping to the extreme left-hand side of the field) down into a dip and then up again. Emerge from this large field crossing a stile and then half left with a fence on the left, to another stile (by double gates) which cross. Then continuing for just a few yards forward, turn right along a rough track which descends for a few yards under an umbrella of trees. On reaching a more major track which comes in from the left continue straight ahead passing a few houses on the right. At the end of the last house turn right into a narrow enclosed path. Ahead and just after this right-hand turn is the public house, The Royal Standard of England, which is amongst the most renowned of country inns in the whole of South-East England.

This enclosed path soon emerges via a stile into a field where keep ahead following the left-hand side of the field. Where the edge of the field bears left continue across the field for about 50 yards to a wooden stile that is plainly visible ahead. Cross this stile into some woods and after about 10 yards at a junction of paths turn left following a clear path which runs firstly just a little inside the woods and then subsequently follows the left-hand edge, eventually emerging into a tarred drive. Follow this drive for a short half mile, and where a house can be seen some 150 yards to the left, turn left where wire fencing ends and keep forward along a fairly clear path which leads ahead with the house on your left and so through a gap in the hedge and out into a partly sunken lane, where you turn right. After about 200 yards you emerge in Penn village with the fine parish church on the left and flintstone cottages on the right. On emerging at the main road, is another popular public house, The Crown.

Turn right at the main road and after a few yards at the end of the public house's car park go forward over a stile and immediately turn sharp left with the perimeter of the car park on your left. The path soon bears left and after a few yards bears right with the substantial beer garden of the pub now on your left. Some thirty yards ahead cross a stile and a few more yards ahead another one into a wood (Vicarage Wood). Follow the clear path gently downhill through this wood emerging after some two hundred yards to a stile with a very large field ahead. Go straight ahead across this field via the clear path encountering on the way a not inconsiderable dip and at the far end go through a gap into some woods. Continue ahead along a clear path which winds its way gently downhill ignoring all turnings to the right and left, eventually emerging at the bottom corner of the woods by a stile, and thence over a field for about 75 yards to another stile and into a road, where you turn right. Keep forward for about 100 yards to a junction of roads at Penn Bottom. At this junction cross the more major road to a stile and proceed straight up some rising ground to a gate which will be seen on the left about 30 yards ahead. Cross the stile to the left of this gate and then immediately turn left along a delightful track that leads uphill through the woods and shrubbery. After about a quarter of a mile this ascending path levels out and becomes a drive with wooden fencing on the left and right. Keep straight along this drive still ascending slightly. The drive shortly joins another (tarred) drive where again continue ahead and on joining a further drive turn left and so for about 400 yards out into the public road where you turn left into the village of Penn Street.

In this village and on the right-hand side there are two excellent public houses, the first of which is the Hit and Miss and the second, a matter of 100 yards further on, The Squirrel. Continue past the public houses with the cricket ground and war memorial on the left, and proceed for about half a mile to a T-junction where you join the main Amersham-High Wycombe road. Turn left at this road and after about 75 yards, turn right where as signposted to Mop End. After bearing to the right and in about 25 yards turn left down a quiet country lane. Then go forward for about a quarter of a mile and just before approaching a farm buildings at Mop End, go right along a clearly signposted footpath and into woods with the edge of a garden of a house on your immediate left and subsequently on, just inside the edge of the woods.

The Squirrel

The path soon bears left by a pylon and from then on, for almost three-quarters of a mile, it really needs no description as it runs clearly down through shrubs, trees, and clearings eventually emerging at a stile. Cross this and then immediately turn left over another stile into a field where you turn right for a few yards and then bear left, continuing downhill with the hedge on your right. Soon you join a track coming in from the right. Follow this track for a few yards and where it bends left continue straight ahead along a (lesser) track with wooded ground on the right. Continue on with the valley bottom just on your right and then with a line of trees on the right and a white house visible ahead. Just before reaching the house the path goes through a kissing gate into a tarred drive upon which continue downhill, eventually passing a cricket ground on your left and emerging at some wrought iron gates. As the road bears left, go forward along a tarred path through some rough ground and so under a bridge (below the by-pass) accompanied by the Misbourne River on your left. The path winds round to the right and becomes a pavement on the left-hand side of the by-pass road.

After about 200 yards the pavement winds its way leftwards and joins the old road, which follows for a short half mile into the centre of Amersham Town. Just after passing the market hall, turn left along Church Street and immediately after passing the church door go to the right along a paved path with the church on the right and the Misbourne River on the left. Cross the river by a humped bridge and immediately turn left and shortly afterwards bear right with the graveyard on your right and continue straight up to a rising field to some woods ahead. (Parsonage Wood). Immediately on entering the wood turn right along a clear path which runs just inside the perimeter of the woods. After passing an opening into a field on the right continue on bearing slightly left with the clear path running on still only some 20 yards inside the perimeter of the wood. Ignore all tracks to the right or left now and continue straight on to a smaller path which soon drops steeply downhill to another track which cross and go forward bearing slightly to the right (still downhill) and out through a gap into the main road where you turn left under the railway bridge and then right into the station approach for Amersham Station.

Route 12: In Deepest Essex

Distance: 5½miles

Map: OS Landranger 168

Start: Marks Tey Station (Great Eastern)

Finish: Chappel and Wakes Colne Station (Great Eastern)

Train service: to Marks Tey half-hourly (hourly on Sundays); from Chappel and Wakes Colne hourly*

As this book goes to press, it has been announced that Sunday services from Chappel and Wakes Colne are suspended indefinitely.

Journey times (minimum): to Marks Tey 46¾miles, 63 minutes; from Chappel and Wakes Colne changing at Marks Tey 50¼ miles, 85 minutes

Ticket: Day return to Chappel and Wakes Colne (Available for leaving train at Marks Tey on outward journey)

Introduction

Essex is a large county as counties go and the contrasts in scenery between one part of the region and another are manifold. This route takes the reader far away from the suburban sprawl that is the feature of West Essex and from the industrial landscapes in the south alongside the Thames Estuary. North Essex is a very pleasant contrast and as part of East Anglia (The Granary of England) it is entirely rural with a low density of population and with such population as there is being concentrated in or around pleasant towns such as Saffron Walden, Braintree and Thaxted, etc.

The locality has been likened to areas of Northern France. Many of the side-roads are unfenced and unhedged reminiscent of the district that lies between and behind the ports of Calais and Boulogne. The starting point at Marks Tey lies a few yards to the north of the A12 trunk road which runs from London to Colchester, where branches lead to the extremity of East Essex (picturesquely known as The

Hundred of Tendring) and the popular seaside resorts of Clacton-on-Sea and Walton-on-the-Naze.

Once away from the noise and bustle of this artery the peace and seclusion of Deepest Essex takes over. The walk encounters only one more classified highway this being the A604, link road from Colchester to Cambridge at the sleepy village of Fordstreet.

At this point, be warned, for it is the only locality passed where refreshment is available, but for good measure the reader will here have the choice of no less than three delightful country inns, or delightful home-made fare at the tea rooms at the Aldham Garden Centre.

Thereafter very remote country is traversed until the conclusion of the walk at Chappel and Wakes Colne station where for a limited number of hours (according to the season) some sustenance is available at the railway museum which forms part of and adjoins the station. Set as it is in the heart of the East Anglian Countryside the museum contains some delightfully nostalgic "railwayana". The British Rail line itself is a quite by-way running from the main line at Marks Tey to the Suffolk market town of Sudbury and here at Chappel and Wakes Colne one is only a few miles south of the Essex/Suffolk border. Years ago, the branch line continued beyond Sudbury to Cambridge but this link from North-East Essex is no longer available. The traveller would nowadays have to travel first to London and then on to Cambridge, a circumlocutory route, but in this age of faster rail travel the trip would probably not take any longer in time, although the distance is effectively doubled.

The walk of some 5½ miles contains nothing in the way of severe gradients – just gentle rises and descents, and can be comfortably covered in a matter of 3 hours (an ideal trip for a summer's evening). Day Return tickets to Chappel and Wakes Colne are of course available for leaving the train at Marks Tey on the outward leg. On the return journey a change of trains is obligatory at Marks Tey for a semi-fast train from there to Liverpool Street in London.

The Journey

Liverpool Street Station where the journey begins is one of London's busiest termini and has recently been refurbished. On leaving Liverpool Street the line ascends through the Shoreditch area and thereafter runs at viaduct level from Bethnal Green to Stratford. This is London's famous East End nowadays consisting mainly of blocks of Council flats but amongst these can still be seen some of the original humble terraces most of which were effectively obliterated from the map during the Blitz of 1940/41.

After having crossed the River Lea and its associated streams (including the oddly named Pudding Mill River) just before reaching Stratford, there follows 10 miles of suburban ribbon development which gradually diminishes as one approaches the market town of Romford. The outer suburbs of Gidea Park and Harold Wood are passed in quick succession giving way to some rural scenery on the approach to the bridge over the M25 ring road and subsequent passing of Brentwood town which is set on a hill.

A stiff climb follows through a deepish cutting to Shenfield where a line to Southend-on-Sea diverges to the right. Next follows Ingatestone, a rural looking station serving a town with an attractive High Street set along the route of a Roman road. The character of the journey then quite dramatically changes into a sizeable area of rural and sparsely populated country. The villages of Mountnessing and Margaretting although close to the railway and on the A12, have never had railway stations and consequently remain rural, and no signs of any extensive habitation are seen until the outskirts of the county capital of Chelmsford, a busy place set around the Rivers Chelmer and Wid.

Hatfield Peverel, Witham and Kelvedon follow. Villages they were but with the asset of fast commuter trains to the City have become small towns, each with their own light industrial developments, and housing estates and in between them attractive areas of East Anglia wheat lands. Marks Tey station which is the start of the walk follows a village that lies some half a mile back to the west of the station itself.

The Walk

On arriving at Marks Tey cross a railway line (with care) into the car park. Emerging from the car park drive turn left and after a short quarter of a mile where the road bends left, continue forward over a stile (just to the left of a letter box) and straight ahead crossing firstly a bridge over the Roman River and then another stile. On entering a large field turn right with the hedge on the right and after some 15 yards where the hedge ends turn left with wire fencing now on your right. Continue in a forward direction at the right-hand side of the field (with the farm buildings of Aldham Hall on your right), and into a small road where bear to the right.

This road is typical of North Essex being mostly hedgeless and running between many acres of cornfields. After about a half a mile one enters the quiet village of Aldham and at the crossroads just before the village church, turn right and go forward with the church on your left. Shortly after the last houses of the village are passed the road then bends sharply to the right. At this point turn left onto an enclosed path (with a ditch on the right and wire fencing on the left). Soon this path veers to the right and continues ahead along an avenue of trees. At the end of the avenue bear right for a few yards and then left and left again through a hedge into another large field with the hedge and a ditch on your right. The path now gently descends into the valley of the river Colne. After a while the hedge on the right ends and the path continues clearly ahead past a lone tree in the middle of the field where shortly afterwards turn sharp left with a house on your right. After a few yards turn right through a gap and out through a drive (with the house on the right) into a road. At this road, turn right. You are now entering the village of Ford Street. On your left is the Aldham Garden Centre where teas and refreshments are served.

On entering the main road turn left through the village. Further facilities for refreshments (and it is quite a long time before you will get any more) are two delightful English Inns, the Coopers Arms on the left and the Queens Head on the right. After crossing the River Colne (which gives its name to neighbouring Colchester) again on the right is a third hostelry, The Shoulder of Mutton.

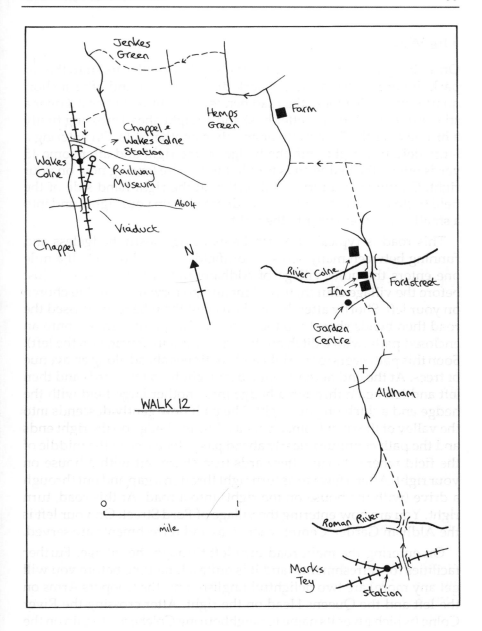

Jerkes
Green

Hemps
Green

Farm

Chappel &
Wakes Colne
Station

Wakes
Colne

Railway
Museum

A604

Viaduct

Chappel

N

River Colne

Fordstreet

Inns

Garden
Centre

Aldham

WALK 12

mile

Roman River

Marks
Tey

Station

At the far end of the village, where the main road to Cambridge turns sharply to the left, keep forward on a minor road signposted to Fordham. After about three hundred yards this road bears sharply to the right. At this point go forward on to a footpath which climbs the bank by a short flight of stairs. On emerging into a large field the way lies straight forward and rising gently uphill. Eventually one comes to a crossing path where you turn left, proceeding downhill crossing a ditch and then rising to join a tiny road where you turn right. After about a quarter of a mile there is a road junction where you turn left and after a further three hundred yards just past a bungalow on the right turn right along a lane, as directed to Hammonds Farm. After about a quarter of a mile and by a willow tree which is on the right of the lane, turn left just before reaching the tree, and cross the edge of a field with a hedge on your right. At the far right-hand end of this field bear right and up and over a bank and slightly left over a plank bridge into the next field where continue ahead with the hedge on your right.

At the far end of this field turn left for about 20 yards and then right across a ditch (there is currently no trace of any bridge remaining) and so ahead over a stile and forward for about 15 yards and over another stile and out into another tiny road. Cross this road and go ahead, continuing along a path which runs clearly along the right-hand side of another large field. Where the hedge on the right ends the path continues along the middle of the field for a few yards and then bears slightly to the right with some wooded ground to the left, followed thereafter by some iron fencing. This path (which is really more of a track) continues straight ahead (with the hedge now on your right) and at the end of the field bends to the left (with another hedge on your right), and so into a small road where you turn left.

After about half a mile this quiet road descends into a dip and immediately after crossing a bridge over a small stream, turn right along a path which follows the right-hand side of a large field. At the corner of the field turn left uphill emerging into a road by some houses. Here go right over a railway bridge and then left downhill for about 100 yards to the entrance to Chappel and Wakes Colne station adjacent to which is the East Anglia Railway Museum.

We publish guides to individual towns, plus books on walking and cycling in the great outdoors throughout England and Wales. This is a recent selection:

South-East Walks and Cycle Rides

BEST PUB WALKS AROUND CENTRAL LONDON – Ruth Herman *(£6.95)*
BEST PUB WALKS IN ESSEX – Derek Keeble *(£6.95)*
LONDON BUS-TOP TOURIST – John Wittich *(£6.95)*
TEA SHOP WALKS IN THE CHILTERNS – Jean Patefield *(£6.95)*
BY-WAY TRAVELS SOUTH OF LONDON – Geoff Marshall *(£6.95)*
BY-WAY BIKING IN THE CHILTERNS – Henry Tindell *(£7.95)*

Walking further afield. . .

FIFTY CLASSIC WALKS IN THE PENNINES – Terry Marsh *(£8.95)*
EAST CHESHIRE WALKS – Graham Beech *(£5.95)*
WEST PENNINE WALKS – Mike Cresswell *(£5.95)*
RAMBLES AROUND MANCHESTER – Mike Cresswell *(£5.95)*
YORKSHIRE DALES WALKING: On The Level – Norman Buckley *(£6.95)*
WELSH WALKS: Dolgellau /Cambrian Coast – L. Main & M. Perrott *(£5.95)*
WELSH WALKS: Aberystwyth & District – L. Main & M. Perrott *(£5.95)*
WALKS IN MYSTERIOUS WALES – Laurence Main *(£7.95)*
RAMBLES IN NORTH WALES – Roger Redfern *(£6.95)*
CHALLENGING WALKS: NW England & N Wales – Ron Astley *(£7.95)*
PUB WALKS IN SNOWDONIA – Laurence Main *(£6.95)*
BEST PUB WALKS AROUND CHESTER & THE DEE VALLEY – John Haywood *(£6.95)*
BEST PUB WALKS IN GWENT – Les Lumsdon *(£6.95)*
PUB WALKS IN POWYS – Les Lumsdon & Chris Rushton *(£6.95)*
BEST PUB WALKS IN PEMBROKESHIRE – Laurence Main *(£6.95)*

More Pub Walks . . .

There are many more titles in our fabulous series of 'Pub Walks' books for just about every popular walking area in the UK, all featuring access by public transport. We label our more recent ones as 'best' to differentiate them from inferior competitors!